101
POTATO
RECIPES

A Collection of Your Favorites

PUBLICATIONS INTERNATIONAL, LTD.

Microwave Cooking: Microwave ovens vary in wattage. Use the cooking times as guidelines and check for doneness before adding more time.

The HEALTHY CHOICE® recipes contained in this book have been tested by the manufacturers and have been carefully edited by the publisher. The publisher and the manufacturers cannot be held responsible for any ill effects caused by errors in the recipes, or by spoiled ingredients, unsanitary conditions, incorrect preparation procedures or any other cause.

101
POTATO
RECIPES
A Collection of Your Favorites

Basic
Potato Facts • 4

Knockout
Appetizers & Starters • 6

Premier
Breakfast & Brunch • 20

Wonderful
Main Dishes • 44

Splendid
Salads • 104

Irresistible
Side Dishes • 124

Flavorful
Soups & Stews • 156

Acknowledgments • 184
Index • 185

Basic POTATO FACTS

Cultivated as early as 3000 B.C. and grown in over a hundred varieties, the potato is easily the most popular vegetable in the United States. In fact, it is estimated that potatoes are included in one-third of all meals that Americans eat.

And we enjoy them in almost as many preparations as there are varieties of potatoes. Mashed potatoes, French fries, potato chips, baked potatoes with sour cream, roasted potatoes, potatoes au gratin, twice-baked potatoes, potato skins . . . the list is endless.

Different potatoes are better for different preparations:

• The **Russet** potato (also known as the Idaho potato) is best for baking, frying and making mashed potatoes.

• The **all-purpose** potato is great for pan-frying, potato pancakes and scalloped potatoes.

• The **Yukon Gold** potato, with its characteristically yellow flesh, is ideal for potato salad and roasted potatoes.

• **Red** potatoes, which have a low starch content, are best for steaming and for grilling.

Potatoes are an ideal food for those people watching their weight. They are very low in calories with virtually no fat and very little sodium. They are also a terrific source of vitamins C and B-1 as well as niacin, potassium and fiber.

Here are a few tips on storing potatoes:

• Keep potatoes at room temperature, preferably in a dark area that is well ventilated.

• After purchasing potatoes, it is best to eat them within 10 days. Be sure to remove them from plastic bags and keep them in a vegetable bin or brown paper bag.

• Potatoes should never be refrigerated, as the starch will convert into sugar.

• Avoid potatoes that have any green coloring to them. This is an indication that they were stored incorrectly and could be bitter as well as potentially toxic in quantity.

• If the potato has sprouted, simply cut out the sprouts before cooking.

Knockout

APPETIZERS & STARTERS

Cheese and Pepper Stuffed Potato Skins

6 large russet potatoes (about ¾ pound each), scrubbed
4 tablespoons FRANK'S® Original REDHOT® Cayenne Pepper Sauce, divided
2 tablespoons butter, melted
1 large red bell pepper, seeded and finely chopped
1 cup chopped green onions
1 cup (4 ounces) shredded Cheddar cheese

1. Preheat oven to 450°F. Wrap potatoes in foil; bake about 1 hour 15 minutes or until fork tender. Let stand until cool enough to handle. Cut each potato in half lengthwise; scoop out insides*, leaving a ¼-inch-thick shell. Cut shells in half crosswise. Place shells on large baking sheet.

2. Preheat broiler. Combine 1 tablespoon RedHot® sauce and butter in small bowl; brush on inside of each potato shell. Broil shells, 6 inches from heat, 8 minutes or until golden brown and crispy.

3. Combine remaining 3 tablespoons RedHot® sauce with remaining ingredients in large bowl. Spoon about 1 tablespoon mixture into each potato shell. Broil 2 minutes or until cheese melts. Cut each piece in half to serve.

Makes 12 servings

*Reserve leftover potatoes for mashed potatoes, home-fries or soup.

Prep Time: 30 minutes
Cook Time: 1 hour 25 minutes

*Cheese and Pepper Stuffed
Potato Skins*

Southwestern Potato Skins

6 large russet potatoes, pierced with fork
¾ pound ground beef
1 package (1.0 ounce) LAWRY'S® Taco
    Spices & Seasonings
¾ cup water
¾ cup sliced green onions
1 medium tomato, chopped
1 can (2¼ ounces) sliced black olives,
    drained
1 cup (4 ounces) shredded Cheddar cheese
2 cups LAWRY'S® Fiesta Dip (recipe
    follows)

Microwave potatoes on HIGH 30 minutes,
turning over after 15 minutes; let cool. Cut in
half and scoop out potatoes leaving ¼-inch shell.
In medium skillet, brown ground beef until
crumbly; drain fat. Stir in Taco Spices &
Seasonings and water. Bring to a boil over
medium-high heat; reduce heat to low and cook,
uncovered, 15 minutes. Stir in green onions.
Spoon meat mixture into potato shells. Top with
tomato, olives and cheese. Place on baking sheet
and heat under broiler to melt cheese. Spoon
dollops of Lawry's Fiesta Dip on each shell.

Makes 1 dozen appetizers

Lawry's® Fiesta Dip

1 package (1.0 ounce) LAWRY'S® Taco
    Spices & Seasonings
1 pint (16 ounces) dairy sour cream

In medium bowl, combine ingredients. Blend
well. Refrigerate until ready to serve.

Makes 2 cups

Cheesy Potato Skins

4 large baking potatoes, baked
¼ cup (½ stick) butter or margarine, melted
¼ pound VELVEETA® Pasteurized Process
    Cheese Spread, cubed
2 tablespoons chopped red or green bell
    pepper
2 slices OSCAR MAYER® Bacon, crisply
    cooked, crumbled
1 tablespoon sliced green onion
    Sour cream

• Heat oven to 450°F.

• Cut potatoes in half lengthwise; scoop out
centers, leaving ¼-inch shells. (Reserve centers
for another use.) Cut shells in half crosswise.
Place on cookie sheet; brush with margarine.

• Bake 20 to 25 minutes or until crisp and
golden brown. Top with process cheese spread;
continue baking until process cheese spread
begins to melt. Top with remaining ingredients.

Makes 16 appetizer servings

Prep Time: 1 hour
Cook Time: 25 minutes

Southwestern Potato Skins

Potato Skins with Cheddar Melt

4 medium-size Idaho baking potatoes (about 2 pounds)
4 slices lean turkey bacon
2 tablespoons vegetable oil
2 cups (8 ounces) shredded ALPINE LACE® Reduced Fat Cheddar Cheese
¼ cup fat free sour cream
2 tablespoons finely chopped chives or green onions
1 tablespoon minced jalapeño pepper

1. Place a piece of foil on the bottom rack of the oven and preheat the oven to 425°F. Scrub the potatoes well and pierce the skins a few times with a sharp knife. Place the potatoes directly on the middle oven rack and bake for 1 hour or until soft.

2. Meanwhile, in a small skillet, cook the bacon over medium heat until crisp. Drain on paper towels, then crumble the bacon.

3. Using a sharp knife, cut the potatoes in half lengthwise. With a small spoon, scoop out the pulp, leaving ¼-inch-thick shells. (Save the potato pulp for another use.) Cut the skins into appetizer-size triangles.

4. Place the skins on a baking sheet, brush the insides with the oil and bake for 15 minutes or until crisp.

5. Remove the skins from the oven, sprinkle with the cheese and return to the oven for 5 minutes or until the cheese melts. Top the skins with the sour cream, then sprinkle with the chives, pepper and bacon.   *Makes about 24 servings*

Cheesy Potato Skins with Black Beans & Salsa

6 medium potatoes (6 ounces each), baked
¾ cup GUILTLESS GOURMET® Black Bean Dip (mild or spicy)
¾ cup (3 ounces) grated Cheddar cheese
¾ cup GUILTLESS GOURMET® Salsa
¾ cup low fat sour cream
Fresh cilantro sprigs (optional)

Preheat oven to 400°F. Cut baked potatoes in half lengthwise and scoop out potato pulp, leaving ¼-inch pulp attached to skin (avoid breaking skin). (Save potato pulp for another use, such as mashed potatoes.) Place potato skins on large baking sheet, skin sides down; bake 5 minutes.

Fill each potato skin with 1 tablespoon bean dip and 1 tablespoon cheese. Return to oven; bake 10 minutes. Remove from oven; let cool 5 minutes. Dollop 1 tablespoon salsa and 1 tablespoon sour cream onto each potato skin. Garnish with cilantro, if desired. Serve hot.

Makes 12 servings

Potato Skins with Cheddar Melt

Potato Pancake Appetizers

3 medium Colorado russet potatoes, peeled and grated
1 egg
2 tablespoons all-purpose flour
1 teaspoon salt
¼ teaspoon black pepper
1½ cups grated zucchini (2 small)
1 cup grated carrot (1 large)
½ cup low-fat sour cream or plain yogurt
2 tablespoons finely chopped fresh basil
1 tablespoon chopped chives *or* 1½ teaspoons chili powder

Preheat oven to 425°F. Wrap potatoes in several layers of paper towels; squeeze to remove excess moisture. Beat egg, flour, salt and pepper in large bowl. Add potatoes, zucchini and carrot; mix well. Oil 2 nonstick baking sheets. Place vegetable mixture by heaping spoonfuls onto baking sheets; flatten slightly. Bake 8 to 15 minutes or until bottoms are browned. Turn; bake 5 to 10 minutes more. Stir together sour cream and herbs; serve with warm pancakes.

Makes about 24 appetizer pancakes

Favorite recipe from **Colorado Potato Administrative Committee**

Zesty Baked Red Potato Fans

6 medium (about 1¼ pounds) red potatoes, unpeeled, scrubbed
Grated peel and juice of 1 SUNKIST® lemon
1 tablespoon olive oil
Salt or garlic salt (optional)
2 tablespoons finely chopped parsley

Cut each potato crosswise but not quite through at ¼-inch intervals. Arrange potatoes in 1½- to 2-quart glass baking dish. Sprinkle with juice of ½ lemon. Cover and microwave on HIGH 6 minutes. Let stand covered for 5 minutes. Drain off any liquid. Sprinkle lemon peel over and between potato slices. Drizzle remaining juice of ½ lemon and olive oil over potatoes. Lightly salt, if desired. Bake, uncovered, at 400°F 30 minutes or until potatoes are tender, brushing potatoes once or twice with any oil in bottom of dish. Sprinkle with parsley. *Makes 3 to 4 servings*

Top to bottom: Colorado Potato Devils (page 152), Hot & Spicy Ribbon Chips (page 14) and Potato Pancake Appetizers

Herbed Potato Chips

    Olive oil-flavored nonstick cooking spray
2 medium-sized red potatoes (about
    ½ pound), unpeeled
1 tablespoon olive oil
2 tablespoons minced fresh dill, thyme or
    rosemary *or* 2 teaspoons dried dill weed,
    thyme or rosemary
¼ teaspoon garlic salt
⅛ teaspoon black pepper
1¼ cups nonfat sour cream

1. Preheat oven to 450°F. Spray large nonstick baking sheets with nonstick cooking spray; set aside. Cut potatoes crosswise into very thin slices, about ¹⁄₁₆ inch thick. Pat dry with paper towels. Arrange potato slices in single layer on prepared baking sheets; coat potatoes with nonstick cooking spray.

2. Bake 10 minutes; turn slices over. Brush with oil. Combine dill, garlic salt and pepper in small bowl; sprinkle evenly onto potato slices. Continue baking 5 to 10 minutes or until potatoes are golden brown. Cool on baking sheets. Serve with sour cream.

Makes about 60 chips

Homemade Potato Chips

    WESSON® Vegetable Oil
2 large russet potatoes, unpeeled
    Salt

Fill a large deep-fry pot or electric skillet to no more than half its depth with Wesson® Oil. Heat oil to 350°F.

Meanwhile, wash and scrub potatoes. Fill a large bowl with cold water three-fourths full. Slice potatoes crosswise into extremely thin pieces (about ¹⁄₁₆ inch); immerse slices in water. Working in small batches, remove potatoes with a slotted spoon; place on paper towels to dry. Fry 2 to 3 minutes or until golden brown and crispy. Remove from oil; drain on paper towels. Immediately salt to taste.

For perfectly golden brown, crispy chips, make sure the oil temperature remains at 350°F.

Makes 4 to 6 servings

Hot & Spicy Ribbon Chips

6 medium unpeeled Colorado russet
    potatoes
1 tablespoon plus 1 teaspoon salt, divided
    Vegetable oil
1 tablespoon chili powder
1 teaspoon garlic salt
¼ to ½ teaspoon ground red pepper

With vegetable peeler, make thin lengthwise potato ribbons. Place in large bowl with 1-quart ice water mixed with 1 tablespoon salt. Heat oil in deep-fat fryer or heavy pan to 365°F. Combine chili powder, remaining 1 teaspoon salt, garlic salt and red pepper; set aside. Drain potatoes and pat dry with paper towels. Fry potatoes in batches until crisp and golden brown; remove with slotted spoon to paper towels. Sprinkle with chili powder mixture. *Makes 8 to 12 servings*

Favorite recipe from **Colorado Potato Administrative Committee**

Herbed Potato Chips

Southern Stuffed New Potatoes with Wisconsin Asiago, Ham and Mushrooms

12 small new red-skinned potatoes (1½ to 2 inches in diameter)
2 tablespoons butter, melted
1 teaspoon butter
2 ounces cooked ham, chopped
¼ cup chopped onion
1 teaspoon chopped fresh thyme
½ teaspoon finely chopped garlic
4 ounces button mushrooms, chopped
2½ ounces portobello mushrooms, chopped*
2½ ounces oyster mushrooms, stemmed and chopped*
3 tablespoons whipping cream
½ cup (2 ounces) shredded Wisconsin Asiago cheese
Salt
Black pepper
½ cup (2 ounces) shredded Wisconsin Baby Swiss cheese
½ cup (2 ounces) shredded Wisconsin medium white Cheddar cheese
¼ cup chopped fresh parsley

*Substitute 5 ounces button mushrooms for portobello and oyster mushrooms, if desired.

Preheat oven to 400°F. Cut ¼ inch off each end of potatoes; discard ends. Cut potatoes in half crosswise. In large bowl, stir together potatoes and 2 tablespoons melted butter until potatoes are well coated.

Place potatoes on parchment-lined 15×10-inch jelly-roll pan. Bake 30 to 40 minutes or until fork tender. Let cool slightly. Scoop out potato pulp, leaving thin shells. Reserve potato pulp for another use. Set shells aside.

Melt 1 teaspoon butter in large skillet over medium-high heat. Add ham; cook 2 to 5 minutes or just until ham begins to brown, stirring occasionally. Add onion, thyme and garlic; decrease heat to medium-low. Cook and stir 2 to 3 minutes or until onion is tender. Add mushrooms. Cook 5 to 6 minutes or until liquid is evaporated, stirring occasionally. Add cream; cook 1 minute, stirring constantly, or until cream is thickened. Stir in Asiago cheese. Season to taste with salt and pepper.

Remove skillet from heat. Meanwhile, in medium bowl, combine Baby Swiss and white Cheddar cheeses; set aside. Fill potato shells with mushroom mixture; sprinkle evenly with Swiss and Cheddar cheese mixture. Cover; refrigerate overnight. To bake, allow potatoes to stand at room temperature 45 minutes. Preheat oven to 400°F. Bake 12 to 15 minutes or until cheeses are melted and lightly browned. Sprinkle with chopped parsley. *Makes 24 appetizers*

Favorite recipe from **Wisconsin Milk Marketing Board**

Spicy Lamb & Potato Nests

POTATO NESTS

2 unpeeled small Colorado potatoes, shredded
1 egg
1 tablespoon vegetable oil
1 tablespoon grated Parmesan cheese
¼ teaspoon garlic powder
¼ teaspoon black pepper
¼ cup biscuit mix
Fine dry bread crumbs

LAMB FILLING

8 ounces lean ground lamb
¼ cup chopped green onion
1 teaspoon grated fresh ginger *or*
¼ teaspoon dry ginger
½ teaspoon ground cumin
¼ teaspoon salt
¼ teaspoon ground coriander
¼ teaspoon ground cinnamon
¼ teaspoon ground red pepper
¼ cup jalapeño pepper jelly

To prepare Potato Nests, place potatoes in medium bowl. Cover with cold water; let stand 5 minutes. Drain well; pat dry with paper towels. Preheat oven to 400°F. Whisk together egg, oil, cheese, garlic powder and black pepper. Stir in biscuit mix until well blended. Stir in shredded potatoes. Generously grease 16 muffin cups; sprinkle bottom of each lightly with bread crumbs. Spoon about 1 tablespoon potato mixture into each cup; make slight indentation in center. Bake 15 minutes. Remove from oven and keep warm.

Meanwhile, to prepare Lamb Filling, cook and stir lamb and onion in saucepan over medium-high heat until lamb is no longer pink and onion is tender. Drain well; add ginger, cumin, salt, coriander, cinnamon and red pepper. Cook and stir 1 to 2 minutes or until flavors are blended. Add jelly; heat until jelly is melted and lamb mixture is heated through. Spoon lamb mixture by rounded teaspoonfuls onto potato nests. Serve hot.   *Makes 16 appetizers*

Favorite recipe from **Colorado Potato Administrative Committee**

Turkey Bacon Quiche in Tater Skins

4 baking potatoes, baked and slightly cooled
4 eggs
8 slices turkey bacon, cooked and crumbled
¼ cup chopped green onions
¼ cup chopped green bell pepper
1 jar (2 ounces) pimientos, drained
½ cup (2 ounces) shredded reduced-fat Cheddar cheese

1. Preheat oven to 350°F. Slice potatoes in half, lengthwise. Scoop out potato pulp, leaving ¼-inch shell. Reserve potato pulp for another use.

2. Combine eggs, bacon, onions, bell pepper and pimientos in medium bowl. Spoon turkey bacon mixture evenly into potato shells; sprinkle with cheese.

3. Bake 15 to 20 minutes or until heated through and cheese is melted.   *Makes 8 servings*

Favorite recipe from **National Turkey Federation**

One Potato, Two Potato

Nonstick cooking spray
2 medium baking potatoes, cut lengthwise
    into 4 wedges
Salt
½ cup unseasoned dry bread crumbs
2 tablespoons grated Parmesan cheese
    (optional)
1½ teaspoons dried oregano leaves, dill weed,
    Italian herbs or paprika
Spicy brown or honey mustard, ketchup
    or reduced-fat sour cream

1. Preheat oven to 425°F. Spray baking sheet with nonstick cooking spray; set aside.

2. Spray cut sides of potatoes generously with cooking spray; sprinkle lightly with salt.

3. Combine bread crumbs, Parmesan cheese and desired herb in shallow dish. Add potatoes; toss lightly until potatoes are generously coated with crumb mixture. Place on prepared baking sheet.

4. Bake potatoes until browned and tender, about 20 minutes. Serve warm as dippers with mustard.
Makes 4 servings

Potato Sweets: Omit Parmesan cheese, herbs and mustard. Substitute sweet potatoes for baking potatoes. Cut and spray potatoes as directed; coat generously with desired amount of cinnamon-sugar. Bake as directed. Serve warm as dippers with peach or pineapple preserves or honey mustard.

Savory Sweet Potato Sticks

3 medium sweet potatoes (about
    1½ pounds)
3 cups KELLOGG'S® RICE KRISPIES®
    cereal, crushed to ¾ cup
½ teaspoon garlic salt
¼ teaspoon onion salt
⅛ teaspoon cayenne pepper
½ cup all-purpose flour
2 egg whites
2 tablespoons water
Vegetable cooking spray
Salsa (optional)

1. Wash potatoes and cut lengthwise into ½-inch slices. Cut slices into ½-inch strips. Set aside.

2. In shallow pan or plate, combine Kellogg's® Rice Krispies® cereal and spices. Set aside. Place flour in second shallow pan or plate. Set aside. Beat together egg whites and water. Set aside. Coat potatoes with flour, shaking off excess. Dip coated potatoes in egg mixture, then coat with cereal mixture. Place in single layer on foil-lined baking sheet coated with cooking spray.

3. Bake at 400°F about 30 minutes or until lightly browned. Serve hot with salsa, if desired.
Makes 15 servings

Prep Time: 25 minutes
Bake Time: 30 minutes

One Potato, Two Potato

BREAKFAST & BRUNCH

Western Omelet

   ½ cup finely chopped red or green bell
      pepper
   ⅓ cup cubed cooked potato
   2 slices turkey bacon, diced
   ¼ teaspoon dried oregano leaves
   2 teaspoons margarine, divided
   1 cup EGG BEATERS® Healthy Real Egg
      Substitute
   Fresh oregano sprig, for garnish

In 8-inch nonstick skillet, over medium heat, sauté bell pepper, potato, turkey bacon and dried oregano in 1 teaspoon margarine until tender.* Remove from skillet; keep warm.

In same skillet, over medium heat, melt remaining margarine. Pour Egg Beaters® into skillet. Cook, lifting edges to allow uncooked portion to flow underneath.

When almost set, spoon vegetable mixture over half of omelet. Fold other half over vegetable mixture; slide onto serving plate. Garnish with fresh oregano.   *Makes 2 servings*

Prep Time: 15 minutes

Cook Time: 10 minutes

*For frittata, sauté vegetables, turkey bacon and dried oregano in 2 teaspoons margarine. Pour Egg Beaters® evenly into skillet over vegetable mixture. Cook without stirring 4 to 5 minutes or until cooked on bottom and almost set on top. Carefully turn frittata; cook 1 to 2 minutes more or until done. Slide onto serving platter; cut into wedges to serve.

Western Omelet

Potato and Pork Frittata

12 ounces (about 3 cups) frozen hash brown
  potatoes
 1 teaspoon Cajun seasoning
 4 egg whites
 2 whole eggs
¼ cup low-fat (1%) milk
 1 teaspoon dry mustard
¼ teaspoon coarsely ground black pepper
10 ounces (about 3 cups) frozen stir-fry
  vegetables
⅓ cup water
¾ cup chopped cooked lean pork
½ cup (2 ounces) shredded Cheddar cheese

1. Preheat oven to 400°F. Spray baking sheet
with nonstick cooking spray. Spread potatoes on
baking sheet; sprinkle with Cajun seasoning.
Bake 15 minutes or until hot. Remove from
oven. *Reduce oven temperature to 350°F.*

2. Beat egg whites, eggs, milk, mustard and
pepper in small bowl. Place vegetables and water
in medium nonstick skillet. Cook over medium
heat 5 minutes or until vegetables are crisp-
tender; drain.

3. Add pork and potatoes to vegetables in skillet;
stir lightly. Add egg mixture. Sprinkle with
cheese. Cook over medium-low heat 5 minutes.
Place skillet in 350°F oven and bake 5 minutes
or until egg mixture is set and cheese is melted.

Makes 4 servings

Frittata Primavera

1 medium onion, chopped
1 medium red or green bell pepper, cut into
  strips
1 medium potato, peeled and grated (about
  1 cup)
1 cup coarsely chopped broccoli
1 teaspoon dried oregano leaves, crushed
⅛ teaspoon ground black pepper
1 tablespoon FLEISCHMANN'S® Original
  Spread (70% Corn Oil)
1 (8-ounce) container EGG BEATERS®
  Healthy Real Egg Substitute

In 10-inch nonstick skillet or omelet pan, cook
and stir onion, bell pepper, potato, broccoli,
oregano and black pepper in spread until
vegetables are tender-crisp.

In small bowl, with electric mixer at high speed,
beat Egg Beaters® for 2 minutes until light and
fluffy; pour over vegetables. Cover and cook over
medium heat for 5 to 7 minutes or until eggs are
set. Serve from pan or carefully invert onto warm
serving plate. Serve immediately.

Makes 4 servings

Potato and Pork Frittata

Zesty Potato Fillo Quiche

2 cups (8 ounces) shredded Jarlsberg Lite™
    cheese
10 large FILLO FACTORY® shells*
1¼ cups diced unpeeled potato (1 large)
1 tablespoon minced garlic
2 teaspoons olive oil
1¼ cups finely chopped green onions
1 egg
3 egg whites
½ cup milk
½ to 1 teaspoon salt
¼ to ½ teaspoon freshly ground black pepper
    Large pinch fresh ground nutmeg
1 to 2 tablespoons snipped fresh dill
    (optional)

*For bite-sized hors d'oeuvres, substitute 30 mini fillo shells.

Microwave Directions: Divide cheese evenly among fillo shells. Arrange shells in microwave oven on paper towel. Microwave at HIGH 1 to 2 minutes, turning every 30 seconds, until cheese is melted. Place fillo shells on cooling rack.

Stir together potato, garlic and oil in 10×6×2-inch glass baking dish. Cover with vented plastic wrap. Microwave at HIGH 3 minutes. Carefully remove plastic wrap and stir in onions. Cover with vented plastic wrap and cook at HIGH 3 minutes. Beat egg and egg whites together in small bowl until blended. Stir in milk, salt, pepper, nutmeg and dill, if desired. Stir into potato mixture. Divide mixture among fillo shells.

Arrange fillo shells in microwave oven on paper towel. Cover with another paper towel. Microwave at HIGH 3 minutes or until filling is set. Carefully remove from oven with spatula. Allow to stand 5 minutes before serving.

Makes 10 servings

Conventional Oven Method: Preheat oven to 350°F. Sauté garlic in oil 3 minutes; add potatoes and sauté 4 minutes. Place fillo shells in paper baking cups in muffin pan. Divide cheese evenly among shells. Mix remaining ingredients in bowl and add potato mixture. Divide mixture evenly among shells. Bake 40 minutes. Remove quiches from muffin pan and baking cups; cool on cooling rack.

Potato and Cheese Omelet

1 teaspoon olive oil
1 small potato, thinly sliced
1 small onion, thinly sliced
1 cup cholesterol-free egg product
½ teaspoon black pepper
1½ cups (6 ounces) HEALTHY CHOICE®
    Fat Free natural shredded Cheddar
    Cheese, divided

In 10-inch nonstick skillet, heat olive oil over medium heat until hot; add potato and onion. Cook and stir until potato is tender. Remove from pan; set aside. In same skillet, add egg product and black pepper. As egg begins to set, run spatula under edge of omelet, lifting cooked portion and allowing uncooked portion to spread to bottom of pan. (Tilt pan as necessary.) When eggs are almost set, sprinkle with 1 cup cheese.

Continue cooking until cheese just begins to melt. Spoon potato-onion mixture on half the omelet. Lift unfilled side of omelet over filling. Sprinkle with remaining ½ cup cheese. To remove from pan, tilt pan slightly; turn omelet onto plate. Serve immediately.

Makes 3 servings

Garden Frittata

1 tablespoon extra-virgin olive oil
1 cup sliced, unpeeled, small red-skinned
   potatoes (about 4 ounces)
½ cup chopped red onion
½ cup chopped red bell pepper
1 teaspoon minced garlic
1 cup chopped fresh asparagus
½ cup fresh corn kernels or frozen corn,
   thawed and drained
1 cup (4 ounces) diced ALPINE LACE®
   Boneless Cooked Ham
¾ cup egg substitute *or* 3 large eggs
3 large egg whites
1 cup (4 ounces) shredded ALPINE LACE®
   Reduced Fat Lightly Smoked Provolone
   Cheese
¼ cup slivered fresh basil leaves *or*
   1 tablespoon dried basil
½ teaspoon salt
¼ teaspoon freshly ground black pepper

1. Preheat the broiler. In a large broilerproof nonstick skillet, heat the oil over medium-high heat. Add the potatoes, onion, bell pepper and garlic. Cook, stirring occasionally, for 7 minutes or until the potatoes are almost tender. Stir in the asparagus, corn and ham and cook 3 minutes more or until the vegetables are crisp-tender.

2. In a medium-size bowl, whisk the egg substitute (or the whole eggs), the egg whites, cheese, basil, salt and black pepper together until blended. Pour over the vegetables. Reduce the heat and cook, uncovered, for 8 minutes or just until the egg mixture is set around the edges.

3. Slide the skillet under the broiler for 1 minute or until the eggs are set in the center. Serve immediately.   *Makes 4 servings*

Hash Brown Frittata

1 (10-ounce) package BOB EVANS®
   Skinless Link Sausage
6 eggs
1 (12-ounce) package frozen hash brown
   potatoes, thawed
1 cup (4 ounces) shredded Cheddar cheese
⅓ cup whipping cream
¼ cup chopped green and/or red bell pepper
¼ teaspoon salt
   Dash black pepper

Preheat oven to 350°F. Cut sausage into bite-size pieces. Cook in small skillet over medium heat until lightly browned, stirring occasionally. Drain off any drippings. Whisk eggs in medium bowl; stir in sausage and remaining ingredients. Pour into greased 2-quart casserole dish. Bake, uncovered, 30 minutes or until eggs are almost set. Let stand 5 minutes before cutting into squares; serve hot. Refrigerate leftovers.

Makes 6 servings

Tamale Potato Quiche

½ pound small red potatoes
1 cup white cornmeal
1 teaspoon ground cumin
¾ teaspoon salt, divided
2 cups (8 ounces) shredded Cheddar cheese, divided
4 eggs, divided
⅓ cup water
2 tablespoons olive oil
½ cup low-fat cottage cheese
2 tablespoons milk
¼ teaspoon ground black pepper
1 can (4 ounces) chopped green chilies, drained
1 medium red bell pepper, seeded and cut into thin strips
Sour cream and fresh cilantro for garnish

1. To prepare potatoes, peel potatoes with vegetable peeler. Cut into ⅛-inch-thick slices.

2. Place in small saucepan; cover with water. Bring to a boil over high heat. Reduce heat to low. Cover and simmer 5 minutes or until potatoes are crisp-tender. Drain. Set aside.

3. Combine cornmeal, cumin, ¼ teaspoon salt and 1 cup Cheddar cheese in medium bowl; toss to mix. Beat 1 egg in small bowl until blended; beat in water and oil until blended. Stir into cornmeal mixture just until cornmeal is moistened.

4. Pat mixture evenly on bottom and up side of greased 9-inch glass pie plate.

5. Place remaining 3 eggs, cottage cheese, milk, remaining ½ teaspoon salt and black pepper in blender; process until smooth.

6. Arrange half of potatoes in layer in crust. Sprinkle with green chilies and ½ cup Cheddar cheese. Top with remaining potatoes and ½ cup Cheddar cheese. Arrange bell pepper strips on top. Carefully pour egg mixture over layers, allowing mixture to seep through layers.

7. Cover completely with plastic wrap, folding ends under. Place round metal cooling rack inside wok; fill wok with 1½ inches water. (Water should not touch rack.) Place pie plate on rack. Bring water to a boil over high heat; reduce heat to low. Cover wok; steam 35 to 40 minutes or until egg mixture is set. (Replenish water, if necessary.)

8. Cool 10 minutes. Cut into wedges. Garnish, if desired.   *Makes 6 servings*

Tamale Potato Quiche

Egg & Sausage Casserole

½ pound pork sausage
3 tablespoons margarine or butter, divided
2 tablespoons all-purpose flour
¼ teaspoon salt
¼ teaspoon black pepper
1¼ cups milk
2 cups frozen hash brown potatoes
4 eggs, hard-boiled and sliced
½ cup cornflake crumbs
¼ cup sliced green onions

Preheat oven to 350°F. Spray 2-quart oval baking dish with nonstick cooking spray.

Crumble sausage into large skillet; brown over medium-high heat until no longer pink, stirring to separate meat. Drain sausage on paper towels. Discard fat and wipe skillet with paper towel.

Melt 2 tablespoons margarine in same skillet over medium heat. Stir in flour, salt and pepper until smooth. Gradually stir in milk; cook and stir until thickened. Add sausage, potatoes and eggs; stir to combine. Pour into prepared dish.

Melt remaining 1 tablespoon margarine. Combine cornflake crumbs and melted margarine in small bowl; sprinkle evenly over casserole.

Bake, uncovered, 30 minutes or until hot and bubbly. Sprinkle with onions.

Makes 6 servings

Hearty Breakfast Custard Casserole

1 pound (2 medium-large) Colorado baking
    potatoes
  Salt and black pepper
8 ounces low-fat bulk pork sausage, cooked
    and crumbled *or* 6 ounces finely diced
    lean ham *or* 6 ounces turkey bacon,
    cooked and crumbled
⅓ cup julienne-sliced roasted red pepper *or*
    1 jar (2 ounces) sliced pimientos,
    drained
3 eggs
1 cup low-fat milk
3 tablespoons chopped fresh chives or green
    onion tops *or* ¾ teaspoon dried thyme
    or oregano leaves
  Salsa and low-fat sour cream or plain
    yogurt (optional)

Heat oven to 375°F. Grease 8- or 9-inch square baking dish or other small casserole. Peel potatoes and slice very thin; arrange half of the potatoes in baking dish. Sprinkle with salt and black pepper. Cover with half of the sausage. Arrange remaining potatoes on top; sprinkle with salt and black pepper. Top with remaining sausage and red peppers. Beat eggs, milk and chives until blended. Pour over potatoes. Cover baking dish with foil and bake 35 to 45 minutes or until potatoes are tender. Uncover and bake 5 to 10 minutes more. Serve with salsa and sour cream, if desired. *Makes 4 to 5 servings*

Favorite recipe from **Colorado Potato Administrative Committee**

Egg & Sausage Casserole

Bratwurst Skillet Breakfast

1½ pounds red potatoes
3 bratwurst links (about ¾ pound)
2 tablespoons butter or margarine
1½ teaspoons caraway seeds
4 cups shredded red cabbage

1. Cut potatoes into ¼- to ½-inch pieces. Place in microwavable casserole. Microwave, covered, on HIGH 3 minutes; stir. Microwave 2 minutes more or until just tender; set aside.

2. While potatoes are cooking, slice bratwurst into ¼-inch pieces. Place bratwurst in large skillet; cook over medium-high heat, stirring occasionally, 8 minutes or until browned and no longer pink in center. Remove bratwurst from pan with slotted spoon; set aside. Pour off drippings.

3. Melt butter in skillet. Add potatoes and caraway. Cook, stirring occasionally, 6 to 8 minutes or until potatoes are golden and tender. Return bratwurst to skillet; stir in cabbage. Cook, covered, 3 minutes or until cabbage is slightly wilted. Uncover and stir 3 to 4 minutes more or until cabbage is just tender yet still bright red.

Makes 4 servings

Serving Suggestion: Serve with fresh fruit and English muffin.

Prep and Cook Time: 30 minutes

Potato and Egg Pie

1 (20-ounce) package frozen O'Brien hash brown potatoes, thawed
⅓ cup WESSON® Vegetable Oil
1½ tablespoons chopped fresh parsley, divided
1 (12-ounce) package bulk breakfast sausage, cooked, crumbled and drained
¾ cup shredded pepper-jack cheese
¾ cup shredded Swiss cheese
1 (4-ounce) can sliced mushrooms, drained
½ cup milk
4 eggs, beaten
1 teaspoon garlic salt
¼ teaspoon black pepper
4 to 6 thin tomato slices

Preheat oven to 425°F. In a medium bowl, combine potatoes and Wesson® Oil; blend to coat. Press mixture into a 10-inch pie dish. Bake for 30 minutes or until golden brown; remove from oven. *Reduce oven temperature to 350°F.* Meanwhile, in a large bowl, combine 1 tablespoon parsley and remaining ingredients except tomato slices; blend well. Pour into potato crust. Bake for 25 minutes or until eggs are set. Place tomato slices over pie and top with remaining parsley. Bake 5 to 7 minutes longer.

Makes 6 servings

Bratwurst Skillet Breakfast

Country Skillet Hash

 2 tablespoons butter or margarine
 4 pork chops (¾ inch thick), diced
 ¼ teaspoon black pepper
 ¼ teaspoon cayenne pepper (optional)
 1 medium onion, chopped
 2 cloves garlic, minced
 1 can (14½ ounces) DEL MONTE®
   FreshCut™ Brand Whole New
   Potatoes, drained and diced
 1 can (14½ ounces) DEL MONTE®
   FreshCut™ Diced Tomatoes, undrained
 1 medium green bell pepper, chopped
 ½ teaspoon dried thyme, crushed

1. Melt butter in large skillet over medium heat. Add meat; cook, stirring occasionally, until no longer pink in center. Season with black pepper and cayenne pepper, if desired.

2. Add onion and garlic; cook until tender. Stir in potatoes, tomatoes, bell pepper and thyme. Cook 5 minutes, stirring frequently. Season with salt, if desired. *Makes 4 servings*

Tip: The hash may be topped with a poached or fried egg.

Prep Time: 10 minutes
Cook Time: 15 minutes

Breakfast Hash

 1 pound BOB EVANS® Special Seasonings
   or Sage Roll Sausage
 2 cups chopped potatoes
 ¼ cup chopped red and/or green bell pepper
 2 tablespoons chopped onion
 6 eggs
 2 tablespoons milk

Crumble sausage into large skillet. Add potatoes, peppers and onion. Cook over low heat until sausage is browned and potatoes are fork-tender, stirring occasionally. Drain off any drippings. Whisk eggs and milk in small bowl until blended. Add to sausage mixture; scramble until eggs are set but not dry. Serve hot. Refrigerate leftovers. *Makes 6 to 8 servings*

Serving Suggestion: Serve with fresh fruit.

Walnut Turkey Hash

4 cups boneless skinless cooked turkey
    chunks
2 medium potatoes, baked and cubed
3 tablespoons butter or margarine
1 cup California walnut pieces
½ cup sliced green onions
1 teaspoon rubbed sage
1 teaspoon dried thyme leaves, crushed
1 cup turkey gravy
    Salt and black pepper to taste
⅓ cup chopped parsley

Combine turkey and potatoes in food processor.
Process until coarsely chopped; set aside. Melt
butter in large skillet. Add walnuts; toss over
medium-low heat until golden brown. Remove
with slotted spoon; set aside. Add onions, sage
and thyme to skillet. Cook and stir 2 minutes.
Add turkey mixture and gravy. Cook and stir
until heated through. Add reserved walnuts, salt
and pepper. Spoon onto serving platter; sprinkle
with parsley.   *Makes 4 to 6 servings*

Favorite recipe from **Walnut Marketing Board**

Spam™ Hash Brown Bake

1 (32-ounce) package frozen hash brown
    potatoes, thawed slightly
½ cup butter or margarine, melted
1 teaspoon salt
1 teaspoon black pepper
½ teaspoon garlic powder
2 cups (8 ounces) shredded Cheddar cheese
1 (12-ounce) can SPAM® Luncheon Meat,
    cubed
1½ cups sour cream
1 (10¾-ounce) can cream of chicken soup
1 (4.25-ounce) jar CHI-CHI'S® Diced
    Green Chilies, drained
½ cup milk
½ cup chopped onion
2 cups crushed potato chips

Heat oven to 350°F. In large bowl, combine
potatoes, melted butter, salt, pepper and garlic
powder. In separate large bowl, combine cheese,
Spam®, sour cream, soup, green chilies, milk and
onion. Add Spam™ mixture to potato mixture;
mix well. Pour into 2-quart baking dish. Sprinkle
with potato chips. Bake 45 to 60 minutes or until
thoroughly heated.   *Makes 8 servings*

Apple-Potato Pancakes

1¼ cups finely chopped unpeeled apples
1 cup grated peeled potatoes
½ cup MOTT'S® Natural Apple Sauce
½ cup all-purpose flour
2 egg whites
1 teaspoon salt
    Additional MOTT'S® Natural Apple
    Sauce or apple slices (optional)

1. Preheat oven to 475°F. Spray cookie sheet with nonstick cooking spray.

2. In medium bowl, combine apples, potatoes, ½ cup apple sauce, flour, egg whites and salt.

3. Spray large nonstick skillet with nonstick cooking spray; heat over medium heat until hot. Drop rounded tablespoonfuls of batter 2 inches apart into skillet. Cook 2 to 3 minutes on each side or until lightly browned. Place pancakes on prepared cookie sheet.

4. Bake 10 to 15 minutes or until crisp. Serve with additional apple sauce or apple slices, if desired. Refrigerate leftovers.

Makes 12 servings

Turkey Sausage Potato Pancakes

1 pound turkey breakfast sausage
1 small onion
2 large potatoes, peeled
½ cup cholesterol-free egg substitute
¼ teaspoon black pepper
    Nonstick cooking spray

1. Cook and stir turkey sausage in large nonstick skillet over medium-high heat 6 to 10 minutes or until sausage is no longer pink. Drain; set aside.

2. Place onion in food processor fitted with metal blade. Process using on/off pulsing action until onion is chopped. Remove metal blade; fit processor with grating disc. Grate potatoes.

3. Combine sausage, potato mixture, egg substitute and pepper in medium bowl until blended. Shape ½ cup sausage mixture into 5-inch round pancake. Repeat with remaining mixture.

4. Spray large nonstick skillet with cooking spray. Heat over medium heat. Cook pancakes 2 to 3 minutes per side or until brown and potatoes are tender. Serve with apple sauce or apple pie filling, if desired. *Makes 4 servings*

Favorite recipe from **National Turkey Federation**

Apple-Potato Pancakes

Potato-Zucchini Pancakes with Warm Corn Salsa

>   Warm Corn Salsa (recipe follows)
>   2 cups frozen hash brown potatoes, thawed
> 1½ cups shredded zucchini, drained
>   ½ cup cholesterol-free egg substitute
>   ¼ cup all-purpose flour
>   2 tablespoons chopped onion
>   2 tablespoons chopped green bell pepper
>   ¼ teaspoon salt
>   ⅛ teaspoon ground black pepper
>   Nonstick cooking spray

1. Prepare Warm Corn Salsa. Keep warm.

2. Combine potatoes, zucchini, egg substitute, flour, onion, bell pepper, salt and black pepper in medium bowl until well blended.

3. Spray large nonstick skillet with cooking spray; heat over medium-high heat until hot. Drop potato mixture by ¼ cupfuls into skillet. Cook pancakes, four or six at a time, about 3 minutes on each side or until golden brown. Place 2 pancakes onto serving plate; top with ½ cup Warm Corn Salsa. Garnish as desired.

Makes 6 servings

Warm Corn Salsa

>   Nonstick cooking spray
>   2 tablespoons chopped onion
>   2 tablespoons finely chopped green bell
>   pepper
>   1 package (9 ounces) frozen whole kernel
>   corn, thawed
>   1 cup chunky salsa
>   2 teaspoons chopped cilantro

1. Spray small nonstick skillet with cooking spray; heat over medium heat until hot. Add onion and bell pepper. Cook and stir 3 minutes or until crisp-tender. Add corn, salsa and cilantro. Reduce heat to medium-low. Cook 5 minutes or until heated through.

Makes 3 cups

Latkes (Potato Pancakes)

> ⅔ cup EGG BEATERS® Healthy Real Egg
>   Substitute
> ⅓ cup all-purpose flour
> ¼ cup grated onion
> ¼ teaspoon ground black pepper
>   4 large potatoes, peeled and shredded (about
>   4 cups)
>   3 tablespoons FLEISCHMANN'S® Original
>   Spread (70% Corn Oil), divided
> 1½ cups sweetened applesauce

In medium bowl, combine Egg Beaters®, flour, onion and pepper; set aside.

Pat shredded potatoes dry with paper towel. Stir into Egg Beaters® mixture. In skillet, over medium-high heat, melt 1½ tablespoons spread. For each pancake, spoon ⅓ cup potato mixture into skillet, spreading into 4-inch circle. Cook 5 to 6 minutes, turning over once to brown both sides. Remove and keep warm. Repeat to make a total of 12 pancakes, using remaining spread as needed. Garnish as desired and serve topped with applesauce.

Makes 12 pancakes

Potato Latkes with Cinnamon Applesauce

INGREDIENTS

Cinnamon Applesauce (recipe follows)
4 medium red potatoes (about 1½ pounds), peeled
2 teaspoons lemon juice
1 small onion, finely chopped
2 eggs, lightly beaten
3 tablespoons all-purpose flour
½ teaspoon salt
¼ teaspoon black pepper
Vegetable oil for frying
Sour cream

SUPPLIES

Pastry bag and medium writing tip

1. Prepare Cinnamon Applesauce; set aside.

2. Shred potatoes into large bowl. Add lemon juice; toss to coat. Drain off excess liquid.

3. Add onion, eggs, flour, salt and pepper to potatoes; mix well.

4. Heat about ¼-inch oil in large skillet over medium-high heat. Spoon about 2 tablespoons potato mixture into oil; spread mixture slightly to make a 3½-inch round. Repeat to form 3 or 4 latkes. Cook 3 to 4 minutes on each side or until golden brown on both sides. Repeat with remaining potato mixture.

5. For individual servings, spoon about 3 tablespoons Cinnamon Applesauce onto small plates; top with 2 latkes. Spoon sour cream into pastry bag fitted with writing tip and pipe onto latkes.   *Makes 6 servings*

Cinnamon Applesauce

1 jar (16 ounces) applesauce
2 tablespoons red cinnamon candies

Combine applesauce and cinnamon candies in small saucepan. Cook over low heat, stirring frequently, until candies are melted and applesauce is heated through.   *Makes 2 cups*

Sweet and Russet Potato Latkes

2 cups shredded russet potato
1 cup shredded sweet potato
1 cup shredded apple
¾ cup cholesterol-free egg substitute
⅓ cup all-purpose flour
1 teaspoon sugar
¼ teaspoon baking powder
¼ teaspoon salt
⅛ teaspoon ground nutmeg
Nonstick cooking spray
1 cup unsweetened cinnamon applesauce

1. Combine potatoes and apple in medium bowl. Combine egg substitute, flour, sugar, baking powder, salt and nutmeg in small bowl; add to potato mixture.

2. Spray large nonstick skillet with cooking spray; heat over medium-low heat until hot. Spoon 1 rounded tablespoonful of potato mixture into skillet to form a pancake about ¼ inch thick and 3 inches in diameter.* Cook 3 minutes or until browned. Turn latke and cook second side 3 minutes or until browned. Repeat with remaining batter. Keep cooked latkes warm in preheated 250°F oven.

3. Top each latke with 1 tablespoon applesauce. Garnish, if desired.   *Makes 8 (2-latke) servings*

*Three to four latkes can be cooked at one time.

Cheesy Potato Pancakes

1½ quarts prepared instant mashed potatoes, cooked dry and cooled
1½ cups (6 ounces) shredded Wisconsin Colby or Muenster cheese
4 eggs, lightly beaten
1½ cups all-purpose flour, divided
¾ cup chopped fresh parsley
⅓ cup chopped fresh chives
1½ teaspoons dried thyme, rosemary or sage leaves
2 eggs, lightly beaten

1. In large bowl, combine potatoes, cheese, 4 beaten eggs, ¾ cup flour and herbs; mix well. Cover and refrigerate at least 4 hours before molding and preparing.

2. To prepare, form 18 (3-inch) patties. Dip in 2 beaten eggs and dredge in remaining ¾ cup flour. Cook and stir each patty in nonstick skillet 3 minutes per side or until crisp, golden brown and heated through.

3. Serve warm with eggs or omelets, or serve with sour cream and sliced pan-fried apples or applesauce.   *Makes 4 to 6 servings*

Variation: Substitute Wisconsin Cheddar or Smoked Cheddar for Colby or Muenster.

Favorite recipe from **Wisconsin Milk Marketing Board**

Sweet and Russet Potato Latkes

Swiss Rosti Potato Cake

2 medium baking potatoes (¾ pound),
    peeled and shredded (about 2 cups)
1⅓ cups (2.8-ounce can) FRENCH'S®
    French Fried Onions, divided
1 small bell pepper (green, red or orange),
    finely chopped
2 teaspoons chopped fresh marjoram *or*
    ½ teaspoon dried marjoram leaves
¼ teaspoon salt
⅛ teaspoon ground black pepper
⅛ teaspoon garlic powder
1 to 2 tablespoons vegetable oil
½ cup (2 ounces) shredded Muenster or
    Swiss cheese

Combine potatoes, ⅔ cup slightly crushed
French Fried Onions, bell pepper, marjoram, salt,
black pepper and garlic powder in medium bowl.

Heat 1 tablespoon oil in heavy 8-inch nonstick
skillet. Spread potato mixture evenly over
bottom of skillet; press down firmly with spatula.
Cook, uncovered, over medium heat 3 minutes
or until bottom is golden.

Loosen potatoes carefully from bottom of skillet
using thin, flexible metal spatula. Place serving
plate over skillet; invert and remove potatoes.
Slide potatoes back into skillet, bottom side up.
If necessary, add remaining oil to skillet to
prevent sticking.

Cook 3 minutes or until golden and potatoes are
cooked through. Sprinkle top with cheese and
remaining ⅔ cup onions. Cover; cook 1 to 2
minutes or until cheese melts. Cut into wedges.
Makes 4 servings

Sweet Potato Biscuits

2½ cups all-purpose flour
¼ cup packed brown sugar
1 tablespoon baking powder
¾ teaspoon salt
¾ teaspoon ground cinnamon
¼ teaspoon ground ginger
¼ teaspoon ground allspice
½ cup vegetable shortening
½ cup chopped pecans
¾ cup mashed canned sweet potatoes
½ cup milk

Preheat oven to 450°F.

Combine flour, sugar, baking powder, salt,
cinnamon, ginger and allspice in medium bowl.
Cut in shortening with pastry blender or 2 knives
until mixture resembles coarse crumbs. Stir in
pecans.

Combine sweet potatoes and milk in separate
medium bowl with wire whisk until smooth.

Make well in center of dry ingredients. Add
sweet potato mixture; stir until mixture forms
soft dough that clings together and forms a ball.

Turn out dough onto well-floured surface. Knead
dough gently 10 to 12 times.

Roll or pat dough to ½-inch thickness. Cut out
dough with floured 2½-inch biscuit cutter.

Place biscuits 2 inches apart on ungreased large
baking sheet. Bake 12 to 14 minutes or until
tops and bottoms are golden brown. Serve warm.
Makes about 12 biscuits

Swiss Rosti Potato Cake

Bayou Yam Muffins

1 cup flour
1 cup yellow cornmeal
¼ cup sugar
1 tablespoon baking powder
1¼ teaspoons ground cinnamon
½ teaspoon salt
2 eggs
1 cup mashed yams or sweet potatoes
½ cup cold strong coffee
¼ cup butter or margarine, melted
½ teaspoon TABASCO® Pepper Sauce

Preheat oven to 425°F. Grease 12 (3×1½-inch) muffin cups. In large bowl combine flour, cornmeal, sugar, baking powder, cinnamon and salt. In medium bowl beat eggs; stir in yams, coffee, butter and TABASCO® Sauce. Make a well in center of dry ingredients; add yam mixture and stir just to combine. Spoon batter into prepared muffin cups. Bake 20 to 25 minutes or until cake tester inserted in center of muffin comes out clean. Cool 5 minutes on wire rack. Remove from pans. Serve warm or at room temperature.   *Makes 12 muffins*

Microwave Directions: Prepare muffin batter as directed above. Spoon approximately ⅓ cup batter into each of 6 paper baking cup-lined 6-ounce custard cups or microwave-safe muffin pan cups. Cook uncovered on HIGH 4 to 5½ minutes or until cake tester inserted in center of muffin comes out clean; turn and rearrange cups or turn muffin pan ½ turn once during cooking. With small spatula, remove muffins. Cool 5 minutes on wire rack. Remove from pans. Repeat procedure with remaining batter. Serve warm or at room temperature.

Sweet Potato Pecan Muffins

MAZOLA NO STICK® Cooking Spray
1¾ cups flour
⅓ cup sugar
2 teaspoons baking powder
1 teaspoon ground cinnamon
½ teaspoon salt
⅛ teaspoon ground nutmeg
¾ cup mashed cooked sweet potatoes
¾ cup KARO® Dark Corn Syrup
⅓ cup MAZOLA® Corn Oil
2 eggs
1 teaspoon vanilla
1 cup chopped pecans

1. Preheat oven to 400°F. Spray 12 (2½-inch) muffin pan cups with cooking spray.

2. In medium bowl, combine flour, sugar, baking powder, cinnamon, salt and nutmeg. In large bowl, with mixer at medium speed, beat sweet potatoes, corn syrup, corn oil, eggs and vanilla until blended. Stir in flour mixture until well blended. Stir in pecans. Spoon into prepared muffin pan cups.

3. Bake 20 minutes or until lightly browned and firm to the touch. Cool in pan on wire rack 5 minutes; remove from pan.   *Makes 12 muffins*

Bayou Yam Muffins

MAIN DISHES

Sunny Day Casserole

1 jar (8 ounces) pasteurized processed
    cheese spread, melted
¾ cup milk
4 cups diced potatoes, partially cooked
2 cups diced HILLSHIRE FARM® Ham
1 package (16 ounces) frozen mixed
    vegetables, thawed
½ cup chopped onion
1 cup (4 ounces) shredded Swiss, Cheddar
    or Monterey Jack cheese
1 cup rich round cracker crumbs

Preheat oven to 350°F.

Combine cheese spread and milk in large bowl.
Stir in potatoes, ham, mixed vegetables and
onion. Pour into medium casserole. Bake,
covered, 45 minutes, stirring occasionally.
Sprinkle Swiss cheese and cracker crumbs over
top. Bake, uncovered, until Swiss cheese is
melted. *Makes 6 servings*

StarKist® Swiss Potato Pie

4 cups frozen shredded hash brown
    potatoes, thawed
2 cups shredded Swiss cheese
1 cup milk
1 can (6 ounces) STARKIST® Solid White
    Tuna, drained and flaked
½ to 1 cup chopped green onions, including
    tops
½ cup chopped green bell pepper (optional)
½ cup sour cream
4 large eggs, beaten
½ teaspoon garlic powder

In large bowl, combine all ingredients. Pour into
lightly greased deep 10-inch pie plate. Bake in
350°F oven 1 hour and 20 minutes or until
golden and crusty. Let stand a few minutes before
slicing into serving portions. *Makes 6 servings*

Sunny Day Casserole

Stuffed Franks 'n Taters

4 cups frozen hash brown potatoes, thawed
1 can (10¾ ounces) condensed cream of
   celery soup
1 cup (4 ounces) shredded Cheddar cheese,
   divided
1 cup sour cream
1⅓ cups (2.8-ounce can) FRENCH'S®
   French Fried Onions, divided
½ teaspoon salt
¼ teaspoon pepper
6 frankfurters

Preheat oven to 400°F. In large bowl, combine potatoes, soup, ½ cup cheese, sour cream, ⅔ cup French Fried Onions and seasonings. Spread potato mixture in 12×8-inch baking dish. Split frankfurters lengthwise almost into halves. Arrange frankfurters, split-side up, along center of casserole. Bake, covered, at 400°F for 30 minutes or until heated through. Fill frankfurters with remaining cheese and ⅔ cup onions; bake, uncovered, 1 to 3 minutes or until onions are golden brown.   *Makes 6 servings*

Microwave Directions: Prepare potato mixture as above; spread in 12×8-inch microwave-safe dish. Cook, covered, on HIGH 8 minutes; stir potato mixture halfway through cooking time. Split frankfurters and arrange on potatoes as above. Cook, covered, 4 to 6 minutes or until frankfurters are heated through. Rotate dish halfway through cooking time. Fill frankfurters with remaining cheese and ⅔ cup onions; cook, uncovered, 1 minute or until cheese melts. Let stand 5 minutes.

Sausage and Potato Bake

1 pound small red new potatoes, cut into
   halves or quarters
1½ cups sliced onions
½ pound baby carrots
2 tablespoons vegetable oil
1 envelope (1¼ ounces) savory herb with
   garlic flavor dry soup mix
1 pound HILLSHIRE FARM® Savory Fare
   Gourmet Cooked Sausage — Chicken
   and Turkey with Apples and Spice,
   diagonally cut into ⅓-inch slices

Preheat oven to 400°F.

Spray 13×9-inch baking pan with nonstick cooking spray. Combine potatoes, onions, carrots, oil and soup mix in large bowl. Stir until evenly coated.

Place potato mixture into prepared pan; bake, uncovered, 30 minutes. Add Gourmet Sausage to potato mixture; stir well. Return pan to oven; bake 15 to 20 minutes or until potatoes are tender and golden brown.

Makes 5 to 6 servings

Sausage and Potato Bake

Ham and Potato au Gratin

3 tablespoons butter or margarine
3 tablespoons all-purpose flour
2 cups milk
1½ cups (6 ounces) shredded Cheddar cheese
1 tablespoon Dijon mustard
2 cups HILLSHIRE FARM® Ham cut into
    thin strips
1 package (24 ounces) frozen shredded hash
    brown potatoes, thawed
1 package (10 ounces) frozen chopped
    spinach, thawed and drained

Preheat oven to 350°F.

Melt butter in large saucepan over medium heat;
stir in flour. Add milk. Cook and stir until
bubbly; cook 1 minute more. Remove from heat.
Stir in cheese and mustard; set aside.

Place ½ of ham into *ungreased* medium casserole.
Top ham with ½ of potatoes and ½ of milk
mixture. Spoon spinach over top. Repeat layers
with remaining ham, potatoes and milk mixture.

Bake, uncovered, 30 minutes or until heated
through.   *Makes 8 servings*

Countdown Casserole

1 jar (8 ounces) pasteurized process cheese
    spread
¾ cup milk
2 cups (12 ounces) cubed cooked roast beef
1 bag (16 ounces) frozen vegetable
    combination (broccoli, corn, red
    pepper), thawed and drained
4 cups frozen hash brown potatoes, thawed
1⅓ cups (2.8-ounce can) FRENCH'S®
    French Fried Onions, divided
½ teaspoon seasoned salt
¼ teaspoon freshly ground black pepper
½ cup (2 ounces) shredded Cheddar cheese

Preheat oven to 375°F. Spoon cheese spread into
12×8-inch baking dish; place in oven just until
cheese melts, about 5 minutes. Using fork, stir
milk into melted cheese until well blended. Stir
in beef, vegetables, potatoes, ⅔ cup French Fried
Onions and seasonings. Bake, covered, at 375°F
30 minutes or until heated through. Top with
Cheddar cheese; sprinkle remaining ⅔ cup
onions down center. Bake, uncovered, 3 minutes
or until onions are golden brown.

Makes 4 to 6 servings

Microwave Directions: In 12×8-inch
microwave-safe dish, combine cheese spread and
milk. Cook, covered, on HIGH 3 minutes; stir.
Add ingredients as directed. Cook, covered, 14
minutes or until heated through, stirring beef
mixture halfway through cooking time. Top with
Cheddar cheese and remaining ⅔ cup onions as
directed. Cook, uncovered, 1 minute or until
cheese melts. Let stand 5 minutes.

Ham and Potato au Gratin

Oven-Easy Beef & Potato Dinner

4 cups frozen hash brown potatoes, thawed
3 tablespoons vegetable oil
⅛ teaspoon pepper
1 pound ground beef
1 cup water
1 package (about ¾ ounce) brown gravy
    mix
½ teaspoon garlic salt
1 package (10 ounces) frozen mixed
    vegetables, thawed and drained
1 cup (4 ounces) shredded Cheddar cheese,
    divided
1⅓ cups (2.8-ounce can) FRENCH'S®
    French Fried Onions, divided

Preheat oven to 400°F. In 12×8-inch baking dish, combine potatoes, oil and pepper. Firmly press potato mixture evenly across bottom and up sides of dish to form a shell. Bake, uncovered, at 400°F for 15 minutes. Meanwhile, in large skillet, brown ground beef; drain. Stir in water, gravy mix and garlic salt; bring to a boil. Add mixed vegetables; reduce heat to medium and cook, uncovered, 5 minutes. Remove from heat and stir in ½ cup cheese and ⅔ cup French Fried Onions; spoon into hot potato shell. *Reduce oven temperature to 350°F.* Bake, uncovered, at 350°F for 15 minutes or until heated through. Top with remaining cheese and ⅔ cup onions; bake, uncovered, 5 minutes or until onions are golden brown. *Makes 4 to 6 servings*

Spinach-Potato Bake

1 pound extra-lean (90% lean) ground beef
½ cup sliced fresh mushrooms
1 small onion, chopped
2 cloves garlic, minced
1 package (10 ounces) frozen chopped
    spinach, thawed and well drained
½ teaspoon grated nutmeg
1 pound russet potatoes, peeled, cooked and
    mashed
¼ cup light sour cream
¼ cup skim milk
    Salt and freshly ground pepper
½ cup (2 ounces) shredded Cheddar cheese

Preheat oven to 400°F. Spray deep 9-inch casserole with nonstick cooking spray.

Brown ground beef in large skillet. Drain. Add mushrooms, onion and garlic; cook until tender. Stir in spinach and nutmeg; cover. Heat thoroughly, stirring occasionally.

Combine potatoes, sour cream and milk. Add to ground beef mixture; season with salt and pepper to taste. Spoon into prepared casserole dish; sprinkle with cheese.

Bake 15 to 20 minutes or until slightly puffed and cheese is melted. *Makes 6 servings*

Chicken-Potato Pot Pie

2 cans (14½ ounces each) chicken broth
1 bay leaf
½ teaspoon white pepper
2 cups cubed Colorado potatoes
1 package (16 ounces) frozen mixed
    vegetables
1 rib celery, chopped
3 tablespoons butter or margarine
3 tablespoons all-purpose flour
3 cups cubed cooked chicken
4 hard-cooked eggs, sliced
    Pastry for 9-inch pie

Combine chicken broth, bay leaf and pepper in large Dutch oven; bring to a boil. Add potatoes; cover, reduce heat to medium and cook 5 minutes. Add frozen vegetables and celery; return to a boil. Cover, reduce heat and simmer 8 to 12 minutes. Remove bay leaf. Drain vegetables, reserving broth. Melt butter in Dutch oven over medium heat; add flour, stirring until smooth. Cook 1 minute, stirring constantly. Gradually add reserved broth; cook, stirring constantly, until mixture is thickened and bubbly. Stir in vegetables, chicken and eggs; spoon mixture into round 2½-quart casserole. Roll out pastry; place over chicken mixture. Trim edges; seal and flute. Roll out dough scraps and cut into decorative shapes, if desired. Dampen pastry cutouts with water and arrange over pastry top. Cut slits in pastry to allow steam to escape. Bake at 400°F for 20 minutes or until golden brown.

Makes 6 to 8 servings

Favorite recipe from **Colorado Potato Administrative Committee**

Creamy Scalloped Potatoes and Tuna

2 cups milk
2 cups whipping cream
2 cloves garlic, minced
2½ pounds (about 6 medium) white or russet
    potatoes
¾ teaspoon salt
½ teaspoon white pepper
1 tablespoon butter or margarine
1 can (12 ounces) STARKIST® Solid White
    or Chunk Light Tuna, drained and
    chunked
1½ cups shredded mozzarella cheese

In 3-quart saucepan over medium heat, heat milk, cream and garlic while preparing potatoes. Peel potatoes; slice about ⅛ to ¼ inch thick. Add potatoes, salt and white pepper to milk mixture; heat to simmering.

Grease 11×7-inch casserole with butter; spoon potato-milk mixture into dish. Bake 25 minutes; remove from oven. Add tuna, stirring gently; top with cheese. Bake 35 more minutes or until potatoes are cooked through and top is golden brown. Let stand, covered, about 15 minutes to thicken.

Makes 6 to 8 servings

Prep Time: 70 minutes

Sausage, Sweet Potato and Apple Casserole

2 sweet potatoes, peeled and cut into 1-inch cubes
2 apples, peeled, cored and cut into 1-inch cubes
1 onion, cut into ⅓-inch strips
2 tablespoons vegetable oil
1 envelope (1¼ ounces) savory herb with garlic flavor dry soup mix
1 pound **HILLSHIRE FARM®** Savory Fare Gourmet Cooked Sausage — Turkey with Scallions and Herbs, diagonally cut into ⅓-inch pieces

Preheat oven to 400°F.

Spray 13×9-inch baking pan with nonstick cooking spray. Combine potatoes, apples, onion, oil and soup mix in large bowl. Stir until evenly coated. Place potato mixture into prepared pan. Bake, covered, 30 minutes. Add Gourmet Sausage to potato mixture; bake 5 to 10 minutes or until sausage is heated through and potatoes are tender.   *Makes 4 to 5 servings*

Baked Apple & Sweet Potato Casserole

6 sweet potatoes
3 apples
2 tablespoons melted butter, divided
½ cup orange juice
¼ cup packed dark brown sugar
¼ cup rum
⅛ teaspoon ground cinnamon
⅛ teaspoon ground allspice

Preheat oven to 350°F. Boil or steam potatoes until tender. Remove skin and cut lengthwise into slices. Peel and core apples; slice into rings. Grease 9×6-inch baking dish with 1 tablespoon butter; alternate potato and apple layers until dish is filled. Pour combined orange juice, sugar, rum, spices and remaining 1 tablespoon butter over potato mixture. Bake 30 minutes or until brown and shiny and liquid is absorbed.

Makes 6 servings

Favorite recipe from **Michigan Apple Committee**

Sausage, Sweet Potato and Apple Casserole

Sweet Potato Turkey Pie

1 can (24 ounces) sweet potatoes, drained
2 tablespoons margarine, melted
¼ teaspoon pumpkin pie spice
    Nonstick vegetable cooking spray
2 cups cubed cooked turkey (½- to ¾-inch
    cubes)
1 can (10¾ ounces) reduced-fat and
    reduced-sodium cream of mushroom
    soup
1 package (9 ounces) frozen French-style
    green beans, thawed and drained
1 can (2 ounces) mushroom stems and
    pieces, drained
½ teaspoon *each* salt and black pepper
2 tablespoons crushed canned French fried
    onions
1 can (8 ounces) cranberry sauce (optional)

1. In medium bowl blend sweet potatoes, margarine and pumpkin pie spice until smooth. Spray 9-inch pie plate with nonstick vegetable cooking spray. Line pie plate with potato mixture to form a "pie shell"; set aside.

2. In medium bowl combine turkey, soup, beans, mushrooms, salt and pepper. Pour mixture into prepared shell. Sprinkle onions over top. Bake at 350°F 30 minutes or until hot. Serve with cranberry sauce, if desired.   *Makes 6 servings*

Favorite recipe from **National Turkey Federation**

Ham & Potato Scallop

1 package (5 ounces) scalloped potatoes plus
    ingredients as package directs
1 bag (16 ounces) BIRDS EYE® frozen
    Broccoli Cuts
½ pound cooked ham, cut into ½-inch cubes
½ cup shredded Cheddar cheese (optional)

• Prepare potatoes according to package directions for stove top method, adding broccoli and ham when adding milk and butter.

• Stir in cheese just before serving.
                                    Makes 4 servings

Serving Suggestion: Spoon mixture into shallow casserole dish. Sprinkle with cheese; broil until lightly browned.

Prep Time: 5 minutes
Cook Time: 25 minutes

Sweet Potato Turkey Pie

Chili & Potato Casserole

1 pound HILLSHIRE FARM® Yard-O-Beef, cut into small cubes
1 cup chopped yellow onion
1 egg, lightly beaten
¼ cup bread crumbs
1 tablespoon chili powder
  Salt to taste
3 cups prepared mashed potatoes
1 can (11 ounces) succotash, drained
¼ cup thinly sliced green onions
1 cup (4 ounces) shredded taco-flavored cheese

Preheat oven to 375°F.

Combine Yard-O-Beef, yellow onion, egg, bread crumbs, chili powder and salt in large bowl; mix thoroughly. Pour beef mixture into medium baking dish, pressing mixture firmly onto bottom of dish. Bake 20 minutes. Pour off any juices.

Mix potatoes, succotash and green onions in medium bowl. Spread potato mixture over beef mixture; sprinkle top with cheese. Broil 3 to 4 inches from heat source 3 to 5 minutes or until top is lightly browned. *Makes 4 to 6 servings*

Shepherd's Pie

2 cups diced cooked leg of American lamb
2 large potatoes, cubed and cooked
2 cups prepared brown gravy
1 cup cooked peas
1 cup cooked carrot slices
3 green onions, sliced
1 clove garlic, minced
1 teaspoon black pepper
2 sheets refrigerated pie crust sheets

In large bowl, combine lamb, potatoes, brown gravy, peas, carrots, green onions, garlic and black pepper.

Press 1 pie crust sheet into 9-inch pie plate; fill with lamb mixture. Cover with second pie crust sheet.* Pinch edges; cut slits in top to allow steam to escape.

Bake 30 minutes at 350°F or until pie crust is golden brown. *Makes 4 to 6 servings*

*Or, use mashed potatoes in place of second crust.

Favorite recipe from **American Lamb Council**

Chili & Potato Casserole

Broccoli and Cheese Topped Potatoes

4 large baking potatoes (6 to 8 ounces each)
2 cups broccoli flowerets
1 cup skim milk
½ cup nonfat cottage cheese
1 teaspoon dry mustard
½ teaspoon red pepper flakes
1 cup (4 ounces) shredded reduced-fat sharp Cheddar cheese, divided
1 cup (4 ounces) shredded part-skim mozzarella cheese
2 tablespoons all-purpose flour

1. Pierce potatoes several times with fork. Place in microwave oven on paper towel. Microwave at HIGH 15 minutes or just until softened. Wrap in paper towels; let stand 5 minutes.

2. Bring water to a boil in medium saucepan over medium heat. Add broccoli. Cook 5 minutes or until broccoli is crisp-tender. Drain and discard water. Add milk, cottage cheese, mustard and red pepper to broccoli in saucepan. Bring to a boil. Reduce heat to medium-low; remove from heat.

3. Combine ¾ cup Cheddar cheese, mozzarella cheese and flour in medium bowl. Toss to coat cheese with flour; add to broccoli mixture. Cook and stir over medium-low heat until cheese is melted and mixture is thickened.

4. Cut potatoes open. Divide broccoli mixture evenly among potatoes. Sprinkle with remaining ¼ cup Cheddar cheese.   *Makes 4 servings*

Microwave Toluca Taters

1 package (1.48 ounces) LAWRY'S® Spices & Seasonings for Chili
1 pound ground turkey
1 can (15¼ ounces) kidney beans, undrained
1 can (14½ ounces) whole peeled tomatoes, undrained and cut up
½ cup water
8 medium russet potatoes, washed and pierced with fork
1 cup (4 ounces) shredded Cheddar cheese
½ cup thinly sliced green onions

Microwave Directions: In large glass bowl, prepare Spices & Seasonings for Chili with ground turkey, kidney beans, tomatoes and water according to package microwave directions; keep warm. Microwave potatoes at HIGH 25 minutes, turning over after 12 minutes. Cut potatoes lengthwise and stir inside with fork to fluff. Top each potato with ½ to ¾ cup prepared chili, 2 tablespoons cheese and 1 tablespoon green onions.   *Makes 8 servings*

Serving Suggestion: Top with sour cream, if desired. Serve with a mixed green salad and fresh fruit.

Hint: This recipe is a great way to use leftover chili.

Broccoli and Cheese
Topped Potatoes

Beef Stroganoff and Zucchini Topped Potatoes

  4 baking potatoes (8 ounces each)
  ¾ pound ground beef round
  ¾ cup chopped onion
  1 cup sliced mushrooms
  2 tablespoons ketchup
  1 beef bouillon cube
  1 teaspoon Worcestershire sauce
  ¼ teaspoon freshly ground black pepper
  ¼ teaspoon hot pepper sauce
  1 medium zucchini, cut into julienned strips
  ½ cup low-fat sour cream, divided

1. Pierce potatoes in several places with fork. Place in microwave oven on paper towel. Microwave potatoes at HIGH 15 minutes or until softened. Wrap in paper towels. Let stand 5 minutes.

2. Heat large nonstick skillet over medium-high heat until hot. Add beef and onion. Cook and stir 5 minutes or until beef is browned. Add all remaining ingredients except zucchini and sour cream. Cover and simmer 5 minutes. Add zucchini. Cover and cook 3 minutes. Remove from heat. Stir in ¼ cup sour cream. Cover and let stand 5 minutes.

3. Cut potatoes open. Divide beef mixture evenly among potatoes. Top with remaining ¼ cup sour cream. *Makes 4 servings*

Prep and Cook Time: 25 minutes

Cheesy Broccoli Potatoes

  6 hot baked potatoes, split lengthwise
  1½ cups chopped cooked broccoli
  1⅓ cups (2.8-ounce can) FRENCH'S®
      French Fried Onions
  ¾ cup pasteurized process American cheese
      sauce, melted

Place potatoes on large microwavable dish. With fork, scrape cooked potato to fluff. Top evenly with broccoli and French Fried Onions. Microwave on HIGH 2 minutes or until onions are golden. Drizzle melted cheese sauce over onions. *Makes 6 servings*

Tip: To bake potatoes quickly, microwave on HIGH 20 to 25 minutes or until tender.

Prep Time: 15 minutes
Cook Time: 2 minutes

Beef Stroganoff and Zucchini Topped Potato

Glazed Chicken & Vegetable Skewers

12 small red or new potatoes (1 pound)
  Golden Glaze (recipe follows)
1 pound skinless boneless chicken thighs or
  breasts, cut into 1-inch pieces
1 yellow or red bell pepper, cut into 1-inch
  pieces
½ small red onion, cut into 1-inch pieces

1. Prepare barbecue grill for direct cooking.

2. Cook potatoes in boiling water until almost
tender, about 10 minutes (or, microwave at
HIGH 3 to 4 minutes or until almost tender).
Rinse with cool water to stop the cooking.

3. Prepare Golden Glaze. Alternately thread
chicken, potatoes, bell pepper and red onion
onto 8 (12-inch) metal skewers. Brush glaze
evenly over both sides of skewered ingredients.

4. Place skewers on grid over medium-hot coals.
Grill, covered, 14 minutes for chicken breast or
16 minutes for chicken thighs or until chicken is
cooked through and vegetables are crisp-tender,
turning once. Season to taste with salt.

Makes 4 servings

Golden Glaze

¼ cup apricot or peach preserves
2 tablespoons spicy brown mustard
2 cloves garlic, minced

1. Combine all ingredients; mix well. Store
tightly covered in refrigerator up to 2 weeks.

Makes about ⅓ cup glaze

Rocky Mountain Hash with Smoked Chicken

1½ pounds Colorado russet variety potatoes,
  unpeeled
2 tablespoons olive oil, divided
1 teaspoon salt, divided
¼ teaspoon black pepper
  Nonstick cooking spray
2 cups chopped red or yellow onions
2 tablespoons bottled minced garlic
2 cups diced red bell peppers
⅛ to ¼ teaspoon cayenne pepper
2 cups shredded smoked chicken or turkey
1 can (11 ounces) whole kernel corn

Cut potatoes into ½- to ¾-inch chunks. Toss
with 1 tablespoon oil, ½ teaspoon salt and black
pepper. Spray 15×10×1-inch baking pan with
nonstick cooking spray. Arrange potato chunks
in single layer; roast at 450°F for 20 to 30
minutes or until tender, stirring and tossing
occasionally. In large skillet heat remaining 1
tablespoon oil. Sauté onions and garlic until
tender. Add bell peppers, remaining ½ teaspoon
salt and cayenne pepper. Cook and stir until
peppers are crisp-tender. Stir in chicken, corn
and potatoes. Cook and stir until heated
through.   *Makes 6 to 8 servings*

Favorite recipe from **Colorado Potato Administrative
Committee**

Snappy Pea and Chicken Pot Pie

2½ cups chicken broth
1 medium-size baking potato, peeled and cut into ½-inch chunks
1½ cups sliced carrots (½-inch slices)
1 cup frozen pearl onions
½ teaspoon dried rosemary
½ teaspoon TABASCO® Pepper Sauce
¼ teaspoon salt
1 medium red bell pepper, coarsely diced
4 ounces (about 1 cup) sugar-snap peas, trimmed and halved lengthwise
3 tablespoons butter or margarine
¼ cup all-purpose flour
8 ounces cooked chicken-breast meat, cut in 3×1-inch strips
1 sheet frozen puff pastry
1 egg, beaten with 1 teaspoon water

In large heavy saucepan bring chicken broth to a boil over high heat. Add potato, carrots, pearl onions, rosemary, TABASCO® Sauce and salt. Reduce heat to medium; cover and simmer 8 to 10 minutes or until vegetables are tender. Add bell pepper and sugar-snap peas; boil 30 seconds, just until peas turn bright green. Drain vegetables, reserving chicken broth; set aside.

Melt butter in saucepan over low heat. Stir in flour and cook 3 to 4 minutes stirring constantly. Pour in 2 cups reserved chicken broth and whisk until smooth. Bring to a boil over medium heat, stirring constantly. Reduce heat to low and simmer 5 minutes, stirring frequently, until thickened and bubbly.

Put chicken strips in bottoms of four lightly buttered ramekins or soufflé dishes. Top chicken with vegetables and sauce.

Heat oven to 475°F.

Thaw pastry and unfold on floured surface according to package directions. Cut pastry into four rectangles. Brush outside rims of ramekins with some of the beaten egg mixture. Place pastry rectangle over each ramekin and press firmly around edges to seal. Trim dough and flute edges. Brush tops with remaining beaten egg mixture.

Place ramekins on baking sheet and bake 10 to 12 minutes, until pastry is puffed and well browned. Serve at once.   *Makes 4 servings*

Hearty Chicken Bake

3 cups hot mashed potatoes
1 cup (4 ounces) shredded Cheddar cheese, divided
1⅓ cups (2.8-ounce can) FRENCH'S® French Fried Onions, divided
1½ cups (7 ounces) cubed cooked chicken
1 package (10 ounces) frozen mixed vegetables, thawed and drained
1 can (10¾ ounces) condensed cream of chicken soup
¼ cup milk
½ teaspoon ground mustard
¼ teaspoon garlic powder
¼ teaspoon pepper

Preheat oven to 375°F. In medium bowl, combine mashed potatoes, ½ cup cheese and ⅔ cup French Fried Onions; mix thoroughly. Spoon potato mixture into greased 1½-quart casserole. Using back of spoon, spread potatoes across bottom and up sides of dish to form a shell. In large bowl, combine chicken, mixed vegetables, soup, milk and seasonings; pour into potato shell. Bake, uncovered, at 375°F for 30 minutes or until heated through. Top with remaining cheese and ⅔ cup onions; bake, uncovered, 3 minutes or until onions are golden brown. Let stand 5 minutes before serving.   *Makes 4 to 6 servings*

Chicken-Vegetable Skillet

8 broiler-fryer chicken thighs, skinned, fat trimmed
¾ teaspoon salt, divided
1 tablespoon vegetable oil
3 medium red-skinned potatoes, scrubbed, cut in ¼-inch slices
1 medium onion, sliced
½ pound mushrooms, quartered
1 large tomato, coarsely chopped
¼ cup chicken broth
¼ cup dry white wine
½ teaspoon dried oregano leaves
¼ teaspoon black pepper
1 tablespoon chopped fresh parsley

Sprinkle chicken with ¼ teaspoon salt. In large nonstick skillet, heat oil to medium-high temperature. Add chicken and cook, turning, about 8 minutes or until brown on both sides. Remove chicken; set aside. In same pan, layer potatoes, onion, chicken, mushrooms and tomato. Mix chicken broth and wine. Pour over chicken and vegetables. Sprinkle with oregano, remaining ½ teaspoon salt and pepper. Heat to boiling; cover and reduce heat to medium-low. Cook about 20 minutes or until chicken and vegetables are fork-tender. Sprinkle with parsley before serving.   *Makes 4 servings*

Favorite recipe from **Delmarva Poultry Industry, Inc.**

Hearty Chicken Bake

Coq au Vin

4 thin slices bacon, cut into ½-inch pieces
6 chicken thighs, skinned
¾ teaspoon dried thyme leaves
1 large onion, coarsely chopped
4 cloves garlic, minced
½ pound small red potatoes, cut into quarters
10 mushrooms, cut into quarters
1 can (14½ ounces) DEL MONTE® *FreshCut*™ Brand Diced Tomatoes with Garlic & Onion
1½ cups dry red wine

1. Cook bacon in 4-quart heavy saucepan until just starting to brown. Sprinkle chicken with thyme; season with salt and pepper, if desired.

2. Add chicken to pan; brown over medium-high heat. Add onion and garlic. Cook 2 minutes; drain.

3. Add potatoes, mushrooms, tomatoes and wine. Cook, uncovered, over medium-high heat about 25 minutes or until potatoes are tender and sauce thickens, stirring occasionally. Garnish with chopped parsley, if desired.

Makes 4 to 6 servings

Prep and Cook Time: 45 minutes

Vesuvio Roasted Chicken and Potatoes

1 chicken (about 3¾ pounds)
⅓ cup olive oil
2 tablespoons fresh lemon juice
4 cloves garlic, minced
3 large baking potatoes, peeled and cut into quarters lengthwise
Salt
Freshly ground black pepper

Preheat oven to 375°F. Place chicken, breast side down, on rack in oiled large shallow roasting pan. Combine oil, lemon juice and garlic in small bowl; brush over chicken. Set aside remaining oil mixture. Bake chicken 30 minutes.

Turn chicken breast side up. Add potatoes to roasting pan. Brush chicken and potatoes with remaining oil mixture; sprinkle with salt and pepper to taste. Bake about 50 minutes or until internal temperature of chicken reaches 180°F on meat thermometer inserted in thickest part of thigh and potatoes are browned and tender. Baste with pan juices each 20 minutes of baking time. Transfer chicken to cutting board; tent with aluminum foil. Let stand 5 to 10 minutes.

Makes 4 to 6 servings

Favorite recipe from **National Foods**

Coq au Vin

Roast Turkey with Sweet Vegetable Purée

¼ **cup parve margarine**
1 **large onion, coarsely chopped**
4 **ribs celery, sliced**
1 **package (11 ounces) dried fruit mix, chopped**
1 **Granny Smith apple, coarsely chopped**
1 **cup slivered almonds or chopped walnuts**
⅓ **cup chopped fresh parsley**
¼ **teaspoon ground cloves**
1 **whole turkey (12 to 14 pounds)**
6 **medium sweet potatoes, peeled, cut into 1-inch pieces**
6 **to 8 carrots, thickly sliced**
5 **large shallots, peeled**
½ **cup kosher dry white wine (optional)**

Preheat oven to 325°F. Melt margarine in large saucepan over medium heat. Add onion; cook, stirring occasionally, 8 minutes or until tender. Remove from heat; stir in celery, fruit mix, apple, almonds, parsley and cloves. Add salt and pepper to taste. Place fruit mixture in turkey cavity. Tie turkey legs together with kitchen string. Place turkey, breast side down, on rack in large oiled roasting pan. Season with salt and pepper, if desired. Add ½ cup water to pan. Bake, uncovered, 1½ hours.

Remove turkey from roasting pan; remove rack. Return turkey, breast side up, to roasting pan. Arrange sweet potatoes, carrots and shallots around turkey; season with salt and pepper, if desired. Baste turkey with pan juices. Add wine to roasting pan, if desired. Bake 2 to 2½ hours or until internal temperature of thigh meat reaches 180°F and legs move easily, basting with pan juices every 30 minutes. Remove turkey to cutting board; tent with foil. Let stand 10 minutes. Remove vegetables from pan with slotted spoon to food processor; process until smooth. Remove fruit stuffing from turkey cavity. Slice turkey. Serve with vegetable purée and fruit stuffing. *Makes 12 servings*

Favorite recipe from **National Foods**

Chicken Vesuvio

1 **whole chicken (about 3¾ pounds)**
¼ **cup olive oil**
3 **tablespoons lemon juice**
4 **cloves garlic, minced**
3 **large baking potatoes, peeled and cut into quarters**
Salt and lemon pepper seasoning

Preheat oven to 375°F. Place chicken, breast side down, on rack in large shallow roasting pan. Combine olive oil, lemon juice and garlic; brush ½ of oil mixture over chicken. Set aside remaining oil mixture. Roast chicken, uncovered, 30 minutes. Turn chicken, breast side up. Arrange potatoes around chicken in roasting pan. Brush chicken and potatoes with remaining oil mixture; sprinkle with salt and lemon pepper seasoning to taste. Roast chicken and potatoes, basting occasionally with pan juices, 50 minutes or until meat thermometer inserted into thickest part of chicken thigh, not touching bone, registers 180°F and potatoes are tender.

Makes 4 to 6 servings

Roast Turkey with Sweet Vegetable Purée

Beef Bourguignon

1 boneless beef sirloin steak, ½ inch thick,
   trimmed and cut into ½-inch pieces
   (about 3 pounds)
½ cup all-purpose flour
4 slices bacon, diced
3 cups Burgundy wine or beef broth
2 medium carrots, diced
1 teaspoon dried marjoram leaves, crushed
½ teaspoon dried thyme leaves, crushed
½ teaspoon salt
   Black pepper to taste
1 bay leaf
2 tablespoons vegetable oil
20 to 24 fresh pearl onions
8 small new red potatoes, cut into quarters
8 to 10 mushrooms, sliced
3 cloves garlic, minced

Coat beef with flour, shaking off excess. Set aside.

Cook and stir bacon in 5-quart Dutch oven over medium-high heat until partially cooked. Brown half of beef with bacon in Dutch oven over medium-high heat. Remove with slotted spoon; set aside. Brown remaining beef. Pour off drippings. Return beef and bacon to Dutch oven. Stir in wine, carrots, marjoram, thyme, salt, pepper and bay leaf. Bring to a boil over high heat. Reduce heat to low. Cover and simmer 10 minutes.

Meanwhile, heat oil in large saucepan over medium-high heat. Cook and stir onions, potatoes, mushrooms and garlic about 10 minutes. Add to Dutch oven. Cover and simmer 50 minutes or until meat is fork-tender. Discard bay leaf before serving.   *Makes 10 to 12 servings*

Malaysian Curried Beef

2 tablespoons vegetable oil
2 large yellow onions, chopped
1 piece fresh ginger (about 1 inch square),
   minced
2 cloves garlic, minced
2 tablespoons curry powder
1 teaspoon salt
2 large baking potatoes (1 pound), peeled
   and cut into 1-inch chunks
1 cup beef broth
1 pound ground beef chuck
2 ripe tomatoes (12 ounces), peeled, seeded
   and chopped
   Hot cooked rice

Heat wok or large skillet over medium-high heat 1 minute or until hot. Drizzle oil into wok. Add onions and stir-fry 2 minutes. Add ginger, garlic, curry and salt to wok. Cook and stir about 1 minute or until fragrant. Add potatoes; cook and stir 3 minutes. Add broth to potato mixture. Cover and bring to a boil. Reduce heat to low; simmer about 20 minutes or until potatoes are fork-tender.

Stir ground chuck into potato mixture. Cook and stir about 5 minutes or until beef is browned and no pink remains; spoon off fat if necessary. Add tomato chunks and stir gently until thoroughly heated. Spoon beef mixture into serving dish. Top center with rice. Garnish as desired.
                              Makes 4 servings

Beef Bourguignon

Herb-Crusted Roast Beef and Potatoes

1 (4½-pound) eye of round or sirloin tip beef roast
¾ cup plus 2 tablespoons FILIPPO BERIO® Olive Oil, divided
2 tablespoons paprika
2 pounds small red skin potatoes, cut into halves
1 cup dry bread crumbs
1 teaspoon dried thyme leaves
1 teaspoon dried rosemary
½ teaspoon salt
¼ teaspoon freshly ground black pepper

Preheat oven to 325°F. Brush roast with 2 tablespoons olive oil. Season to taste with salt and pepper. Place in large roasting pan; roast 45 minutes.

Meanwhile, in large bowl, combine ½ cup olive oil and paprika. Add potatoes; toss until lightly coated. In small bowl, combine bread crumbs, thyme, rosemary, ½ teaspoon salt, ¼ teaspoon pepper and remaining ¼ cup olive oil.

Carefully remove roast from oven. Place potatoes around roast. Press bread crumb mixture onto top of roast to form crust. Sprinkle any remaining bread crumb mixture over potatoes. Roast an additional 40 to 45 minutes or until meat thermometer registers 145°F for medium-rare or until desired doneness is reached. Transfer roast to carving board; tent with foil. Let stand 5 to 10 minutes before carving. Cut into ¼-inch-thick slices. Serve immediately with potatoes, spooning any bread crumb mixture from roasting pan onto meat. *Makes 8 servings*

Savory Pot Roast

⅔ cup A.1.® Original or A.1.® Bold & Spicy Steak Sauce
1 (0.9-ounce) envelope dry onion-mushroom soup mix
1 cup water, divided
1 (2½-pound) boneless beef chuck roast
6 medium potatoes, quartered
6 medium carrots, peeled, cut into 1-inch pieces
2 tablespoons all-purpose flour

In small bowl, blend steak sauce, soup mix and ¾ cup water; set aside.

Line shallow baking pan or dish with heavy-duty foil, overlapping edges. Place roast in center of foil; place potatoes and carrots around roast. Pour steak sauce mixture evenly over beef and vegetables. Seal foil loosely over top of beef; secure side edges tightly. Bake at 350°F 2 hours or until beef is tender. Remove beef to heated serving platter. Using slotted spoon, remove vegetables to same platter; keep warm. Remove and discard foil.

For gravy, dissolve flour in remaining ¼ cup water. Stir into pan liquid; cook until thickened, stirring occasionally. Slice beef; serve with vegetables and gravy. *Makes 8 servings*

Herb-Crusted Roast Beef and Potatoes

Masaman Curry Beef

Masaman Curry Paste (recipe follows) *or*
½ cup canned Masaman curry paste
2 pounds boiling potatoes
4 tablespoons vegetable oil, divided
1 medium onion, cut into strips
1½ pounds boneless beef chuck or round, cut
  into 1-inch pieces
2 cans (about 14 ounces each) unsweetened
  coconut milk
3 tablespoons fish sauce
1 large red bell pepper, cut into strips
½ cup roasted peanuts, chopped
2 tablespoons lime juice
¼ cup slivered fresh basil leaves or chopped
  cilantro

1. Prepare Masaman Curry Paste; set aside.

2. Peel potatoes and cut into 1½-inch pieces. Place in bowl with cold water to cover; set aside.

3. Heat 1 tablespoon oil in wok or large skillet over medium-high heat. Add onion; stir-fry 6 to 8 minutes or until golden. Transfer onion to bowl with slotted spoon.

4. Add 1 tablespoon oil to wok. Increase heat to high. Add half the beef; stir-fry 2 to 3 minutes or until browned on all sides. Transfer beef to another bowl; set aside. Repeat with remaining beef, adding 1 tablespoon oil to prevent sticking if necessary.

5. Reduce heat to medium. Add remaining 1 tablespoon oil and curry paste to wok; cook and stir 1 to 2 minutes or until very fragrant. Add coconut milk and fish sauce; stir to scrape bits of cooked meat and spices from bottom of wok.

6. Return beef to wok. Increase heat to high and bring to a boil. Reduce heat to low; cover and simmer 45 minutes or until meat is fork-tender.

7. Drain potatoes; add to wok with onion. Cook 20 to 30 minutes more or until potatoes are fork-tender. Stir in bell pepper; cook 1 to 2 minutes more or until pepper is heated through.

8. Stir in peanuts and lime juice. Pour into serving bowl and sprinkle with basil. Serve with rice or noodles and garnish, if desired.

Makes 6 servings

Masaman Curry Paste

Grated peel of 2 lemons
6 tablespoons coarsely chopped ginger
3 tablespoons coarsely chopped garlic (10 to
  12 cloves)
2 tablespoons ground cumin
2 tablespoons ground mace or nutmeg
4 teaspoons packed brown sugar
2 teaspoons ground cinnamon
2 to 4 teaspoons ground red pepper*
2 teaspoons paprika
2 teaspoons black pepper
2 teaspoons anchovy paste *or* 1 minced
  anchovy fillet
1 teaspoon turmeric
1 teaspoon ground cloves

*Use 2 teaspoons ground red pepper for mild paste and up to 4 teaspoons for very hot paste.

Place all ingredients in food processor or blender; process until mixture forms dry paste.

Makes about ½ cup

Masaman Curry Beef

Meat and Potato Stir-Fry

1 tablespoon vegetable oil
1 large baking potato, peeled and cut into ½-inch cubes
2 medium carrots, peeled and thinly sliced
1 medium onion, halved and sliced
⅔ cup beef broth
1 teaspoon salt, divided
1 pound lean ground round
1 large clove garlic, minced
1 tablespoon dried parsley flakes
1 teaspoon paprika
½ teaspoon ground cinnamon
½ teaspoon ground cumin
¼ teaspoon black pepper

1. Heat oil in wok or large skillet over medium-high heat until hot. Add potato, carrots and onion; cook and stir 3 minutes. Stir in beef broth and ½ teaspoon salt. Reduce heat to medium. Cover and cook 6 to 7 minutes or until potato is tender, stirring once or twice. Remove vegetables from wok; set aside. Wipe out wok with paper towel.

2. Heat wok over medium-high heat until hot. Add beef and garlic; stir-fry 3 minutes or until meat is no longer pink. Add parsley, paprika, cinnamon, cumin, remaining ½ teaspoon salt and pepper; cook and stir 1 minute. Add vegetables; heat through. *Makes 4 servings*

Prep and Cook Time: 25 minutes

Classic Brisket Tzimmes

2 first cut (about 2½ pounds each) or 1 whole HEBREW NATIONAL® Fresh Brisket (about 5 to 6 pounds), well trimmed
2 tablespoons vegetable oil
1 large onion, chopped
3 cloves garlic, minced
2 cups beef or chicken broth
½ cup orange juice
2 tablespoons light brown sugar
2 tablespoons fresh lemon juice
1 tablespoon tomato paste
1 teaspoon dried thyme leaves
1 teaspoon ground cinnamon
¼ teaspoon ground cloves
6 to 8 medium carrots, peeled, sliced
3 sweet potatoes, peeled, sliced
8 ounces dried pitted prunes

Preheat oven to 325°F. Place brisket in large roasting pan; sprinkle with salt and pepper. Heat oil in medium saucepan over medium-high heat. Add onion and garlic; cook and stir 8 minutes. Stir in broth, orange juice, brown sugar, lemon juice, tomato paste, thyme, cinnamon and cloves. Bring to a boil, stirring occasionally. Pour evenly over brisket. Cover; bake 1½ hours. Add carrots, sweet potatoes and prunes to pan. Cover; bake 1 to 1½ hours or until brisket and vegetables are fork-tender. Transfer brisket to cutting board; tent with foil. Spoon pan juices over fruit and vegetables; transfer to serving platter. Skim fat from pan juices; discard fat. Slice brisket across the grain into ¼-inch-thick slices; transfer to serving platter. Spoon sauce over brisket and vegetables. *Makes 10 to 12 servings*

Meat and Potato Stir-Fry

Cowboy Kabobs

½ cup A.1.® Original or A.1.® Bold & Spicy
  Steak Sauce
½ cup barbecue sauce
2½ teaspoons prepared horseradish
1 (1½-pound) beef top round steak, cut into
  ½-inch strips
4 medium-size red skin potatoes, cut into
  wedges, blanched
1 medium onion, cut into wedges
⅓ cup red bell pepper strips
⅓ cup green bell pepper strips
⅓ cup yellow bell pepper strips

Soak 8 (10-inch) wooden skewers in water at
least 30 minutes.

In small bowl, combine steak sauce, barbecue
sauce and horseradish; set aside.

Alternately thread steak strips (accordion style)
and vegetables onto skewers. Place kabobs in
nonmetal dish; coat with ⅔ cup reserved steak
sauce mixture. Cover; refrigerate 1 hour, turning
occasionally.

Remove kabobs from marinade; discard
marinade. Grill kabobs over medium heat or
broil 6 inches from heat source 6 to 10 minutes
or until steak is desired doneness, turning
occasionally and basting with remaining steak
sauce mixture. Serve immediately.

Makes 4 servings

Grilled Meat Loaves and Potatoes

1 pound ground beef
½ cup A.1.® Original or A.1.® Bold & Spicy
  Steak Sauce, divided
½ cup plain dry bread crumbs
1 egg, beaten
¼ cup finely chopped green bell pepper
¼ cup finely chopped onion
2 tablespoons margarine, melted
4 (6-ounce) red skin potatoes, blanched,
  sliced into ¼-inch-thick rounds
Grated Parmesan cheese
Additional A.1.® Original or A.1.® Bold
  & Spicy Steak Sauce (optional)

In large bowl, combine beef, ¼ cup steak sauce,
bread crumbs, egg, pepper and onion. Shape into
4 (4-inch) oval loaves; set aside.

In small bowl, combine remaining ¼ cup steak
sauce and margarine; set aside.

Grill meat loaves over medium heat 20 to 25
minutes and potato slices 10 to 12 minutes or
until beef is no longer pink in center and
potatoes are tender, turning and basting both
occasionally with reserved steak sauce mixture.
Sprinkle potatoes with cheese. Serve
immediately with additional steak sauce, if
desired.   *Makes 4 servings*

Cowboy Kabobs

Potato-Crusted Meat Loaf

1 large yellow onion
1 large green bell pepper
1 large red bell pepper
3 large cloves garlic
1 pound lean ground beef
1 pound ground veal
¼ cup egg substitute *or* 1 large egg, beaten
½ cup bottled chili sauce
1 cup seasoned dry bread crumbs, divided
½ cup (2 ounces) shredded ALPINE LACE®
    Fat Free Pasteurized Process Skim Milk
    Cheese Product—For Cheddar Lovers
½ teaspoon freshly ground black pepper
1 pound russet baking potatoes, peeled,
    cooked, kept hot (2 large)
1 cup (4 ounces) shredded ALPINE LACE®
    Fat Free Pasteurized Process Skim Milk
    Cheese Product—For Cheddar Lovers
¼ cup minced chives
2 tablespoons unsalted butter substitute,
    melted

1. Preheat the broiler. Place the onion, bell peppers and garlic cloves on a baking sheet. Broil 3 inches from heat for 7 minutes or until blackened, turning frequently. Transfer to a paper bag, close tightly and let stand 15 minutes or until soft. Scrape off outside skins. Chop the onion and garlic; seed and chop the peppers. (You will have about 2 cups vegetables.)

2. Preheat the oven to 350°F and spray a 13×9×3-inch baking dish with nonstick cooking spray. In a large bowl, mix the beef, veal, vegetables, egg substitute (or the whole egg), chili sauce, bread crumbs, the ½ cup of the cheese and the black pepper. Mix with your hands until well combined. Transfer to the baking dish and pat into a 12×7-inch loaf, mounding it slightly in the center.

3. In a small bowl, with an electric mixer set on medium-high, whip the hot potatoes with the 1 cup of cheese, the chives and the butter until fluffy. Pipe or spoon on top and sides of the loaf. Bake for 1 hour or until a meat thermometer inserted into the center of the meat loaf registers 145°F. Let stand for 10 minutes, then serve.

Makes 12 servings

Potato Topped Meat Loaf

1 jar (12 ounces) HEINZ® HomeStyle
    Mushroom or Beef Gravy
1½ pounds lean ground beef
1 cup soft bread crumbs
¼ cup finely chopped onion
1 egg, slightly beaten
½ teaspoon salt
    Dash pepper
2½ cups hot mashed potatoes
1 tablespoon melted butter or margarine
    Paprika

Measure ¼ cup gravy from jar; combine with beef, bread crumbs, onion, egg, salt and pepper. Shape into 8×4×1½-inch loaf in shallow baking pan. Bake in 350°F oven 1 hour. Remove from oven and carefully drain fat. Spread potatoes over top and sides of meat loaf. Drizzle melted butter over potatoes; garnish with paprika. Return meat loaf to oven; bake an additional 20 minutes. Let stand 5 minutes. Heat remaining gravy and serve with meat loaf slices.   *Makes 6 servings*

Potato-Crusted Meat Loaf

Patchwork Casserole

2 pounds ground beef
2 cups chopped green bell peppers
1 cup chopped onion
2 pounds frozen southern-style hash brown
    potatoes, thawed
2 cans (8 ounces each) tomato sauce
1 cup water
1 can (6 ounces) tomato paste
1 teaspoon salt
½ teaspoon dried basil, crumbled
¼ teaspoon ground black pepper
1 pound pasteurized process American
    cheese, thinly sliced

Preheat oven to 350°F.

Cook and stir beef in large skillet over medium heat until crumbled and brown, about 10 minutes; drain off fat.

Add bell peppers and onion; cook and stir until tender, about 4 minutes. Stir in potatoes, tomato sauce, water, tomato paste, salt, basil and black pepper.

Spoon ½ mixture into 13×9×2-inch baking pan or 3-quart baking dish; top with half of cheese. Spoon remaining meat mixture evenly on top of cheese. Cover pan with aluminum foil. Bake 45 minutes.

Cut remaining cheese into decorative shapes; place on top of casserole. Let stand loosely covered until cheese melts, about 5 minutes.

Makes 8 to 10 servings

Family Favorite Hamburger Casserole

1 tablespoon CRISCO® Vegetable Oil
1 cup chopped onion
1 pound ground beef round
1 package (9 ounces) frozen cut green beans
3 cups frozen southern-style hash brown
    potatoes
1 can (10¾ ounces) zesty tomato soup
½ cup water
1 teaspoon dried basil leaves
¾ teaspoon salt
¼ teaspoon black pepper
¼ cup plain dry bread crumbs

1. Heat oven to 350°F. Oil 11¾×7½×2-inch baking dish lightly.

2. Heat Crisco® Oil in large skillet on medium-high heat. Add onion. Cook and stir until tender. Add meat. Cook until browned, stirring occasionally. Add beans. Cook and stir 5 minutes or until thawed. Add potatoes.

3. Combine tomato soup and water in small bowl. Stir until well blended. Stir into skillet. Stir in basil, salt and pepper. Spoon into baking dish. Sprinkle with bread crumbs.

4. Bake at 350°F for 30 minutes or until potatoes are tender. Let stand 5 minutes before serving.

Makes 4 servings

Patchwork Casserole

Irish Stew in Bread

1½ pounds lean, boned American lamb
    shoulder, cut into 1-inch cubes
¼ cup all-purpose flour
2 tablespoons vegetable oil
2 cloves garlic, crushed
2 cups water
¼ cup Burgundy wine
5 medium carrots, chopped
3 medium potatoes, peeled and sliced
2 large onions, peeled and chopped
2 ribs celery, sliced
¾ teaspoon black pepper
1 beef bouillon cube, crushed
1 cup frozen peas
¼ pound fresh sliced mushrooms
    Round bread, unsliced*

*Stew may be served individually or in one large loaf. Slice bread crosswise near top to form lid. Hollow larger piece, leaving 1-inch border. Fill "bowl" with hot stew; cover with "lid." Serve immediately.

Coat lamb with flour while heating oil over low heat in Dutch oven. Add lamb and garlic; cook and stir until brown. Add water, wine, carrots, potatoes, onions, celery, pepper and bouillon. Cover; simmer 30 to 35 minutes.

Add peas and mushrooms. Cover; simmer 10 minutes. Bring to a boil; correct seasonings, if necessary. Serve in bread.

Makes 6 to 8 servings

Favorite recipe from **American Lamb Council**

Lamb in Dill Sauce

2 large boiling potatoes, peeled and cut into
    1-inch cubes
½ cup chopped onion
1½ teaspoons salt
½ teaspoon black pepper
½ teaspoon dried dill weed *or* 4 sprigs fresh
    dill
1 bay leaf
2 pounds lean lamb stew meat, cut into
    1-inch cubes
1 cup plus 3 tablespoons water, divided
2 tablespoons all-purpose flour
1 teaspoon sugar
2 tablespoons lemon juice
    Fresh dill (optional)

Slow Cooker Directions: Layer ingredients in slow cooker in the following order: potatoes, onion, salt, pepper, dill, bay leaf, lamb and 1 cup water. Cover and cook on LOW 6 to 8 hours.

Remove lamb and potatoes with slotted spoon; cover and keep warm. Remove and discard bay leaf. Turn heat to HIGH. Stir flour and remaining 3 tablespoons water in small bowl until smooth. Add half of cooking juices and sugar. Mix well and return to slow cooker. Cover and cook 15 minutes. Stir in lemon juice. Return lamb and potatoes to slow cooker. Cover and cook 10 minutes or until heated through. Garnish with fresh dill, if desired.

Makes 6 servings

Irish Stew in Bread

Grilled Pork and Potatoes Vesuvio

1 center-cut boneless pork loin roast
  (1½ pounds), well trimmed and cut into
  1-inch cubes
½ cup dry white wine
2 tablespoons olive oil
4 cloves garlic, minced, divided
1½ to 2 pounds small red potatoes (about
  1½ inches in diameter), scrubbed
6 metal skewers (12 inches long)
6 lemon wedges
  Salt (optional)
  Black pepper (optional)
¼ cup chopped fresh Italian or curly leaf
  parsley
1 teaspoon finely grated lemon peel

1. Place pork in large resealable plastic food storage bag. Combine wine, oil and 3 cloves garlic in small bowl; pour over pork.

2. Place potatoes in single layer in microwave-safe dish. Pierce each potato with tip of sharp knife. Microwave at HIGH 6 to 7 minutes or until almost tender when pierced with fork. (Or, place potatoes in large saucepan. Cover with cold water. Bring to a boil over high heat. Simmer about 12 minutes or until almost tender when pierced with fork.) Immediately rinse with cold water; drain. Add to pork in bag. Seal bag tightly, turning to coat. Marinate in refrigerator at least 2 hours or up to 8 hours, turning occasionally.

3. Prepare barbecue grill for direct cooking.

4. Meanwhile, drain pork mixture; discard marinade. Alternately thread about 3 pork cubes and 2 potatoes onto each skewer. Place 1 lemon wedge on end of each skewer. Sprinkle salt and pepper over pork and potatoes, if desired.

5. Place skewers on grid. Grill skewers, on covered grill, over medium coals 14 to 16 minutes or until pork is juicy and barely pink in center and potatoes are tender, turning halfway through grilling time.

6. Remove skewers from grill. Combine parsley, lemon peel and remaining minced garlic clove in small bowl. Sprinkle over pork and potatoes. Squeeze lemon wedges over pork and potatoes.

Makes 6 servings

Grilled Pork and Potatoes Vesuvio

Pork and Cabbage Ragout

1 tablespoon vegetable oil
1 pound pork tenderloin, cut into scant
    ½-inch slices
1 cup chopped onion
4 cloves garlic, minced
1½ teaspoons crushed caraway seeds
8 cups thinly sliced cabbage (1 pound) or
    prepared coleslaw mix
1 cup dry white wine
1 teaspoon chicken bouillon crystals
2 medium Cortland or Jonathan apples,
    peeled and cut into wedges
**Instant potato flakes plus ingredients to
    prepare 4 servings mashed potatoes**

1. Heat oil in large saucepan over medium heat until hot. Add pork; cook and stir about 2 minutes per side or until browned and barely pink in center. Sprinkle lightly with salt and pepper. Remove from saucepan and reserve. Add onion, garlic and caraway to saucepan; cook and stir 3 to 5 minutes or until onion is tender.

2. Add cabbage, wine and chicken bouillon to saucepan; bring to a boil. Reduce heat to low; simmer, covered, 5 minutes or until cabbage is wilted. Cook over medium heat, uncovered, 5 to 8 minutes or until excess liquid is gone.

3. Add apple wedges and reserved pork; cook, covered, 5 to 8 minutes or until apples are tender. Season to taste with salt and pepper. While ragout is cooking, prepare potatoes according to package directions. Serve ragout over potatoes.   *Makes 4 (1-cup) servings*

Savory Pork Chop Supper

6 medium potatoes, thinly sliced (about
    5 cups)
1⅓ cups (2.8-ounce can) FRENCH'S®
    French Fried Onions, divided
1 jar (2 ounces) sliced mushrooms, drained
2 tablespoons butter or margarine
¼ cup soy sauce
1½ teaspoons ground mustard
½ teaspoon FRANK'S® Original REDHOT®
    Cayenne Pepper Sauce
⅛ teaspoon garlic powder
1 tablespoon vegetable oil
6 pork chops, ½ to ¾ inch thick

Preheat oven to 350°F. In 12×8-inch baking dish, layer half the potatoes and ⅔ cup French Fried Onions. Top with mushrooms and remaining potatoes. In small saucepan, melt butter; stir in soy sauce, mustard, cayenne pepper sauce and garlic powder. Brush half the soy sauce mixture over potatoes. In large skillet, heat oil. Brown pork chops on both sides; drain. Arrange chops over potatoes and brush with remaining soy sauce mixture. Bake, covered, at 350°F for 1 hour. Bake, uncovered, 15 minutes or until pork chops and potatoes are done. Top chops with remaining ⅔ cup onions; bake, uncovered, 5 minutes or until onions are golden brown.
          Makes 4 to 6 servings

Pork and Cabbage Ragout

Skillet Franks and Potatoes

3 tablespoons vegetable oil, divided
4 HEBREW NATIONAL® Quarter Pound
    Dinner Beef Franks or 4 Beef
    Knockwurst
3 cups chopped cooked red potatoes
1 cup chopped onion
1 cup chopped seeded green bell pepper or
    combination of green and red bell
    peppers
3 tablespoons chopped fresh parsley
    (optional)
1 teaspoon dried sage leaves
½ teaspoon salt
¼ teaspoon freshly ground black pepper

Heat 1 tablespoon oil in large nonstick skillet over medium heat. Score franks; add to skillet. Cook franks until browned. Transfer to plate; set aside.

Add remaining 2 tablespoons oil to skillet. Add potatoes, onion and bell pepper; cook and stir about 12 to 14 minutes or until potatoes are golden brown. Stir in parsley, sage, salt and pepper.

Return franks to skillet; push down into potato mixture. Cook about 5 minutes or until heated through, turning once halfway through cooking time. *Makes 4 servings*

Classic Potato, Onion & Ham Pizza

3 tablespoons butter or olive oil, divided
3 cups new potatoes, cut into ¼-inch slices
2 sweet onions, cut into ¼-inch slices
1 tablespoon coarsely chopped garlic
½ teaspoon salt
½ teaspoon black pepper
2 cups (8 ounces) shredded Wisconsin
    Mozzarella cheese
1 (16-ounce) Italian-style bread shell pizza
    crust
8 thin slices (4 ounces) deli ham
8 slices (4 ounces) Wisconsin Provolone
    cheese
⅓ cup grated Wisconsin Parmesan cheese
¼ cup chopped Italian parsley

Melt 2 tablespoons butter in large skillet over medium heat; add potatoes, onions, garlic, salt and pepper. Cook 12 to 15 minutes, turning occasionally. Add remaining 1 tablespoon butter. Cook 5 to 7 minutes or until potatoes are golden brown. Cool slightly.

Preheat oven to 400°F. Sprinkle mozzarella cheese over crust; top with ham slices. Arrange potato mixture over ham; top with Provolone cheese. Sprinkle with Parmesan cheese and parsley. Place crust directly on oven rack; bake 15 to 20 minutes or until cheese is melted. *Makes 4 servings*

Favorite recipe from **Wisconsin Milk Marketing Board**

Skillet Franks and Potatoes

Country Kielbasa Kabobs

½ cup GREY POUPON® COUNTRY
  DIJON® Mustard
½ cup apricot preserves
⅓ cup minced green onions
 1 pound kielbasa, cut into 1-inch pieces
 1 large apple, cored and cut into wedges
½ cup frozen pearl onions, thawed
 6 small red skin potatoes, parboiled and cut
  into halves
 3 cups shredded red and green cabbage,
  steamed

Soak 6 (10-inch) wooden skewers in water 30
minutes. In small bowl, blend mustard, preserves
and green onions; set aside ¼ cup mixture.

Alternately thread kielbasa, apple, pearl onions
and potatoes on skewers. Grill or broil kabobs 12
to 15 minutes or until done, turning and
brushing with remaining mustard mixture. Heat
reserved mustard mixture and toss with steamed
cabbage. Serve hot with kabobs. Garnish as
desired.   *Makes 6 servings*

Turkey Kielbasa with Cabbage, Sweet Potatoes and Apples

 1 bottle (12 ounces) dark beer or ale
 2 tablespoons Dijon mustard
½ teaspoon caraway seeds
 6 cups coarsely shredded cabbage
 1 pound fully cooked turkey kielbasa or
  smoked turkey sausage, cut into 2-inch
  pieces
 1 can (16 ounces) sweet potatoes, cut into
  1½-inch cubes
 1 Granny Smith apple, cut in ¼-inch
  wedges

1. Combine beer, mustard and caraway seeds in
large deep skillet. Bring to a boil over high heat.
Add cabbage. Reduce heat to medium-low.
Cover and cook 5 to 8 minutes or until cabbage
is crisp-tender.

2. Add kielbasa, sweet potatoes and apple.
Increase heat to high. Bring mixture to a boil.
Reduce heat to medium-low. Cover and cook 3
to 5 minutes or until apple is crisp-tender.
                                            Makes 6 servings

Favorite recipe from **National Turkey Federation**

Country Kielbasa Kabobs

German-Style Bratwurst & Sauerkraut

6 slices bacon
1 small onion, chopped
1 clove garlic, minced
1 (32-ounce) jar or can sauerkraut, rinsed
    and well drained
2 medium potatoes, peeled and sliced
1½ to 2 cups water
½ cup apple juice or dry white wine
2 tablespoons brown sugar
1 teaspoon instant chicken bouillon granules
1 teaspoon caraway seeds
1 dried bay leaf
1 pound BOB EVANS® Bratwurst (5 links)
2 medium apples, cored and sliced
    Fresh bay leaves (optional)

Cook bacon in large skillet over medium-high heat until crisp. Remove bacon; drain and crumble on paper towel. Set aside. Drain off all but 2 tablespoons drippings in skillet. Add onion and garlic to drippings; cook over medium heat until tender, stirring occasionally. Stir in sauerkraut, potatoes, 1½ cups water, juice, brown sugar, bouillon, caraway and dried bay leaf. Add remaining ½ cup water, if necessary, to cover potatoes. Bring to a boil over high heat.

Meanwhile, make 3 or 4 diagonal ¼-inch-deep cuts into one side of each bratwurst. Cook bratwurst in large skillet over medium heat until browned, turning occasionally. Add bratwurst to sauerkraut mixture. Reduce heat to low; simmer, covered, 20 to 30 minutes or until potatoes are just tender, stirring occasionally.

Add apples; cook, covered, 5 to 10 minutes or until apples are just tender. Stir in reserved bacon. Remove and discard dried bay leaf. Garnish with fresh bay leaves, if desired. Serve hot. Refrigerate leftovers.　　*Makes 5 servings*

Kielbasa Kabobs

½ cup A.1.® Steak Sauce
¼ cup GREY POUPON® Dijon Mustard
3 tablespoons light molasses
2 tablespoons cider vinegar
1 tablespoon vegetable oil
1 clove garlic, minced
1 teaspoon cornstarch
1 pound kielbasa, sliced into 1-inch pieces
6 small red skin potatoes, parboiled and cut
    into wedges (about 12 ounces)
1 medium onion, cut into wedges
1 medium apple, cut into wedges
    Steamed shredded red and green cabbage

Soak 6 (10-inch) wooden skewers in water for at least 30 minutes. In small saucepan, blend steak sauce, mustard, molasses, vinegar, oil, garlic and cornstarch. Over medium heat, cook and stir until sauce thickens and begins to boil; cool.

Alternately thread kielbasa, vegetables and apple onto skewers. Grill kabobs over medium heat for 12 to 15 minutes or until done, turning and brushing often with prepared sauce. Serve hot with prepared cabbage.　　*Makes 6 servings*

German-Style Bratwurst &
Sauerkraut

Baked Fish with Potatoes and Onions

1 pound baking potatoes, very thinly sliced
1 large onion, very thinly sliced
1 small red or green bell pepper, thinly
   sliced
Salt
Black pepper
½ teaspoon dried oregano leaves, divided
1 pound lean fish fillets, cut 1 inch thick
¼ cup butter or margarine
¼ cup all-purpose flour
2 cups milk
¾ cup (3 ounces) shredded Cheddar cheese

Preheat oven to 375°F.

Arrange ½ potatoes in buttered 3-quart casserole. Top with ½ onion and ½ bell pepper. Season with salt and black pepper. Sprinkle with ¼ teaspoon oregano. Arrange fish in 1 layer over vegetables. Arrange remaining potatoes, onion and bell pepper over fish. Season with salt, black pepper and remaining ¼ teaspoon oregano.

Melt butter in medium saucepan over medium heat. Stir in flour; cook until bubbly, stirring constantly. Gradually stir in milk. Cook until thickened, stirring constantly. Pour white sauce over casserole. Cover and bake at 375°F 40 minutes or until potatoes are tender. Sprinkle with cheese. Bake, uncovered, about 5 minutes more or until cheese is melted.

Makes 4 servings

Fish Tajin (Fish Braised in Olive Oil with Vegetables)

3 tablespoons FILIPPO BERIO® Olive Oil
4 small potatoes, peeled and cut into
   ⅛-inch-thick slices
2 large red bell peppers, seeded and cut into
   strips
3 small tomatoes, peeled and chopped
1 jalapeño pepper, seeded and chopped
   or ½ teaspoon chili powder
3 cloves garlic, minced
2 pounds fish steaks, 1 inch thick (cod,
   haddock, halibut or skate)
1 tablespoon lime or lemon juice
½ cup chopped fresh cilantro

In large skillet or Dutch oven, heat olive oil over medium heat until hot. Carefully layer potatoes in pan; simmer gently 5 minutes. Add bell peppers, tomatoes, jalapeño pepper and garlic; mix well. Add fish, spooning vegetable mixture over fish. Cover; reduce heat to low and cook 10 to 15 minutes or until fish flakes easily when tested with fork. Sprinkle with lime juice. Top with cilantro.

Makes 8 servings

*Baked Fish with Potatoes
and Onions*

Fish & Chips

¾ cup all-purpose flour
½ cup flat beer or lemon-lime carbonated
    beverage
Vegetable oil
4 medium russet potatoes, each cut into
    8 wedges
Salt
1 egg, separated
1 pound cod fillets
Malt vinegar (optional)

Combine flour, beer and 2 teaspoons oil in small bowl. Cover; refrigerate 1 to 2 hours.

Pour 2 inches of oil into heavy skillet. Heat oil over medium heat until a fresh bread cube placed in oil browns in 45 seconds (about 365°F). Add as many potato wedges as will fit. Do not crowd. Fry potato wedges 4 to 6 minutes or until outsides are brown, turning. Drain on paper towels; sprinkle lightly with salt. Repeat with remaining potato wedges. (Allow temperature of oil to return to 365°F between frying batches.) Reserve oil to fry cod.

Stir egg yolk into flour mixture. Beat egg white with electric mixer at high speed in bowl until soft peaks form. Fold egg white into flour mixture; set aside. Rinse fish and pat dry with paper towels. Cut fish into 8 pieces. Dip 4 fish pieces into batter; fry 4 to 6 minutes or until batter is crispy and brown and fish flakes easily when tested with fork, turning once. Drain on paper towels. Repeat with remaining fish pieces.

(Allow temperature of oil to return to 365°F between frying batches.) Serve immediately with potato wedges. Sprinkle fish with malt vinegar, if desired. Garnish as desired.   *Makes 4 servings*

New West Crab Cakes

1 pound crabmeat
¾ pound Idaho potatoes, mashed (or 1 cup
    instant mashed potatoes)
1 cup bread crumbs, divided
½ cup chopped California Walnuts, divided
⅓ cup chopped red onion or chives
2 egg whites
1 egg yolk
Pinch salt

Combine crabmeat, potatoes, ½ cup bread crumbs, ¼ cup walnuts, onion, egg whites, egg yolk and salt in medium bowl. Form into 8 flat patties. Mix together remaining ½ cup bread crumbs and ¼ cup finely chopped walnuts. Coat crab patties with bread crumb mixture. Cook over medium heat in skillet brushed with oil.

Serve with lemon wedges or fresh tomato relish made with chopped green and yellow peppers, red onion and diced, seeded tomatoes, seasoned with salt and pepper to taste. Or, substitute prepared salsa.   *Makes 4 servings*

Favorite recipe from **Walnut Marketing Board**

Baked Fish Galician Style

½ cup plus 4 teaspoons FILIPPO BERIO®
    Olive Oil, divided
1 large onion, chopped
2 tablespoons minced fresh parsley, divided
2 cloves garlic, crushed
2 teaspoons paprika
1½ pounds new potatoes, peeled and cut into
    ⅛-inch-thick slices
1 tablespoon all-purpose flour
3 small bay leaves
½ teaspoon dried thyme leaves
    Dash ground cloves
4 orange roughy or scrod fillets, 1 inch
    thick (about 2 pounds)
    Salt and freshly ground black pepper
    Lemon wedges (optional)

Preheat oven to 350°F. In large skillet, heat ½ cup olive oil over medium heat until hot. Add onion; cook and stir 5 to 7 minutes or until softened. Stir in 1 tablespoon parsley, garlic and paprika. Add potatoes; stir until lightly coated with mixture. Sprinkle with flour. Add enough water to cover potatoes; stir gently to blend. Add bay leaves, thyme and cloves. Bring to a boil. Cover; reduce heat to low and simmer 20 to 25 minutes or until potatoes are just tender. (*Do not overcook potatoes.*)

Spoon potato mixture into 1 large or 2 small casseroles. Place fish fillets on top of potato mixture. Drizzle 1 teaspoon of remaining olive oil over each fillet. Spoon sauce from bottom of casserole over each fillet.

Bake 15 to 20 minutes or until fish flakes easily when tested with fork. Sprinkle fillets with remaining 1 tablespoon parsley. Season to taste with salt and pepper. Remove bay leaves before serving. Serve with lemon wedges, if desired.

Makes 4 servings

New England Fisherman's Skillet

4 small red potatoes, diced
1 medium onion, chopped
1 tablespoon olive oil
2 stalks celery, chopped
2 cloves garlic, minced
½ teaspoon dried thyme, crushed
1 can (14½ ounces) DEL MONTE®
    Original Recipe Stewed Tomatoes
1 pound firm white fish (such as halibut,
    snapper or cod)

1. Brown potatoes and onion in oil over medium-high heat in large skillet, stirring occasionally. Season with herb seasoning mix, if desired.

2. Stir in celery, garlic and thyme; cook 4 minutes. Add tomatoes; bring to a boil. Cook 4 minutes or until thickened.

3. Add fish; cover and cook over medium heat 5 to 8 minutes or until fish flakes easily with fork. Garnish with lemon wedges and chopped parsley, if desired.

Makes 4 servings

Prep Time: 10 minutes
Cook Time: 25 minutes

Grilled Tuna Niçoise

4 tuna steaks, 1 inch thick (about 1½ pounds)
2 tablespoons FRENCH'S® Worcestershire Sauce
2 tablespoons olive oil

NIÇOISE DRESSING

½ cup prepared olive oil vinaigrette salad dressing
¼ cup FRENCH'S® Dijon Mustard
¼ cup sour cream
1 tablespoon capers, drained
2 cloves garlic, minced

SALAD

6 cups washed and torn mixed gourmet baby lettuce leaves
8 small (12 ounces) red potatoes, cooked and sliced
2 ripe tomatoes, cut into wedges
1 small seedless cucumber, sliced
½ pound green beans, cooked until tender
½ cup oil-cured black olives

Place tuna steaks on large platter. Combine Worcestershire and oil in cup; brush on both sides of steaks.

Place steaks on oiled grid. Grill over hot coals 10 minutes or until fish is opaque, but still feels somewhat soft in center,* turning once. Remove from grill.

To prepare Niçoise Dressing, combine salad dressing, mustard, sour cream, capers and garlic in small bowl; mix well. To serve, arrange lettuce, tuna steaks, potatoes, tomatoes, cucumber, beans and olives on individual salad plates, dividing evenly. Serve with Niçoise Dressing. *Makes 4 servings*

*Tuna becomes dry and tough if overcooked. Watch carefully while grilling.

Variation: For Tangy Fish Sauce, combine ½ cup mayonnaise and 2 tablespoons French's® Dijon Mustard. Stir in 1 tablespoon chopped capers or pickle relish. Serve with your favorite grilled fish.

Tip: Potatoes and green beans cook easily in microwave. Place sliced potatoes and beans in 3-quart microwave-safe baking dish. Pour 1 cup water over vegetables. Cover and microwave on HIGH 12 minutes or until vegetables are tender, stirring once. Drain and cool.

Prep Time: 30 minutes
Cook Time: 10 minutes

Sweet Potato Ravioli with Asiago Cheese Sauce

¾ pound sweet potato
2 tablespoons plain nonfat yogurt
1 teaspoon minced fresh chives
1 tablespoon plus ¼ teaspoon minced fresh sage, divided
24 wonton wrappers
1 tablespoon reduced-calorie margarine
1 tablespoon plus 2 teaspoons all-purpose flour
½ cup skim milk
½ cup ⅓-less-salt chicken broth
½ cup (2 ounces) shredded Asiago or Cheddar cheese
¼ teaspoon ground nutmeg
¼ teaspoon ground white pepper
⅛ teaspoon ground cinnamon

1. Preheat oven to 350°F. Bake sweet potato 40 to 45 minutes or until tender. Cool completely. Peel potato and mash pulp. Stir in yogurt, chives and ¼ teaspoon sage.

2. Place wonton wrappers on counter. Spoon 1 rounded teaspoon potato mixture in center of each wonton. Spread filling flat leaving ½-inch border. Brush edges lightly with water. Fold wontons in half diagonally, pressing lightly to seal. Place filled wontons on baking sheet and cover loosely with plastic wrap.

3. Bring 1½ quarts water to a boil in large saucepan. Reduce heat to medium. Add a few ravioli at a time. (Do not overcrowd.) Cook until tender, about 9 minutes. Transfer to platter with slotted spoon.

4. Melt margarine in small saucepan. Stir in flour; cook 1 minute, stirring constantly. Gradually stir in milk and chicken broth. Cook and stir until slightly thickened, about 4 minutes. Stir in cheese, nutmeg, white pepper and cinnamon.

5. Spoon 3 tablespoons sauce onto individual plates. Place 3 ravioli onto each plate. Sprinkle with remaining sage.   *Makes 8 servings*

Maple Spam™ Stuffed Squash

3 small acorn squash (about 1 pound each), cut in half, seeds removed
½ cup chopped celery
¼ cup chopped onion
2 tablespoons butter or margarine
1 (12-ounce) can SPAM® Luncheon Meat, chopped
1½ cups frozen cubed hash brown potatoes, thawed
½ cup chopped apple
¼ cup pure maple syrup or maple-flavored syrup

Heat oven to 375°F. Place squash, cut side up, in 13×9-inch baking pan. In large skillet over medium-high heat, sauté celery and onion in butter until tender. Stir in Spam® and potatoes. Cook, stirring occasionally, until potatoes are lightly browned. Stir in apple and syrup. Spoon ½ cup Spam™ mixture into each squash half. Cover. Bake 40 to 50 minutes or until squash is tender.   *Makes 6 servings*

Sweet Potato Ravioli with Asiago Cheese Sauce

Splendid SALADS

Green Bean and Potato Salad in Dijon Vinaigrette

Dijon Vinaigrette (recipe follows)
1½ pounds small red-skinned potatoes
10 ounces fresh green beans
1 cup quartered cherry tomatoes
½ cup chopped onion
⅛ teaspoon salt
⅛ teaspoon black pepper

1. Prepare Dijon Vinaigrette; set aside.

2. Place potatoes in 3-quart saucepan; cover with water. Bring to a boil over medium-high heat. Reduce heat to low; simmer, covered, 10 to 15 minutes until fork-tender. Drain potatoes in colander. Rinse under cold running water; drain. Cut potatoes lengthwise into halves; set aside.

3. Rinse beans thoroughly in colander under cold running water; drain. Snap off stem end from each bean; discard. Cut beans into 2-inch pieces. Place beans in 2-quart saucepan; cover with water. Bring to a boil over medium-high heat.

4. Reduce heat to low; simmer, covered, 5 to 6 minutes until beans are crisp-tender. Transfer beans to colander; rinse under cold running water. Drain; set aside.

5. Combine potatoes, beans, tomatoes and onion in large bowl. Add Dijon Vinaigrette, salt and pepper; toss well. Cover tightly with plastic wrap. Refrigerate 2 to 3 hours.   *Makes 6 servings*

Dijon Vinaigrette

3 tablespoons honey-Dijon mustard
Juice of ½ lemon
2 tablespoons red wine vinegar
1 clove garlic, minced
½ teaspoon Worcestershire sauce
⅓ cup extra-virgin olive oil

1. In small bowl, combine mustard, lemon juice, vinegar, garlic and Worcestershire; whisk to blend. Gradually whisk in oil.   *Makes ⅔ cup*

*Green Bean and Potato Salad in
Dijon Vinaigrette*

Country-Style Sausage Potato Salad

3 pounds red potatoes, cut into 1-inch
  chunks, boiled until tender and drained
2 tablespoons cider vinegar, divided
1 (9-ounce) HILLSHIRE FARM® Summer
  Sausage, cut lengthwise into quarters,
  then sliced
2 tablespoons packed brown sugar
2 tablespoons Dijon mustard
1 tablespoon olive oil
½ teaspoon salt
½ teaspoon black pepper
½ cup sliced green onions
¼ cup chopped parsley

Place warm potatoes in serving bowl; toss with 1 tablespoon vinegar. Cook Summer Sausage in medium skillet over medium heat until nearly crisp, about 5 minutes; drain and set aside. Combine brown sugar, mustard, oil, remaining 1 tablespoon vinegar, salt and pepper in small bowl. Pour brown sugar mixture, sausage, onions and parsley over potatoes; toss to mix. Serve warm.   *Makes 10 to 12 side-dish servings*

Walnut Sweet Potato Salad

2 pounds sweet potatoes or yams, boiled just
  until tender and drained
⅓ cup vegetable oil
2 tablespoons cider vinegar
1 tablespoon soy sauce
1 teaspoon finely grated fresh ginger
1 small clove garlic, minced
1 large red apple, cored and sliced
½ cup sliced green onions
⅔ cup toasted walnut pieces
  Black pepper to taste
  Butter lettuce

Cool potatoes completely; set aside. Meanwhile, whisk together oil, vinegar, soy sauce, ginger and garlic in large bowl. Add apple and onions; toss. Peel and cut sweet potatoes into ¼-inch-thick slices; add with walnuts to apple mixture. Toss gently. Season with pepper. Arrange lettuce on serving platter. Spoon potato mixture onto lettuce. Garnish with additional apple slices, if desired. Serve at room temperature.
                    Makes 6 servings

Favorite recipe from **Walnut Marketing Board**

Country-Style Sausage Potato Salad

Hot German Potato Salad

1½ pounds new or boiling-type potatoes, cut into ¾-inch cubes
1⅓ cups water, divided
½ teaspoon salt
½ pound bacon, cut crosswise into thin strips
2 tablespoons cider vinegar
4 teaspoons sugar
1 tablespoon FRENCH'S® Worcestershire Sauce
2 teaspoons cornstarch
¼ teaspoon ground black pepper
1⅓ cups (2.8-ounce can) FRENCH'S® French Fried Onions, divided
1 cup chopped green bell pepper
1 cup chopped celery
¼ cup chopped pimento

Microwave Directions: Place potatoes, 1 cup water and salt in 3-quart microwave-safe dish. Cover and microwave on HIGH 15 minutes or until potatoes are tender, stirring once. Drain in colander; set aside.

Place bacon in same dish. Microwave, uncovered, on HIGH 5 minutes or until bacon is crisp, stirring once. Remove bacon with slotted spoon; set aside. Pour off all but ¼ cup bacon drippings. Stir in remaining ⅓ cup water, vinegar, sugar, Worcestershire, cornstarch and black pepper. Microwave, uncovered, on HIGH 1 to 2 minutes or until dressing has thickened, stirring once.

Return potatoes to dish. Add ⅔ cup French Fried Onions, bell pepper, celery, pimento and reserved bacon; toss well to coat evenly. Microwave, uncovered, on HIGH 2 minutes. Stir. Sprinkle with remaining ⅔ cup onions. Microwave on HIGH 1 minute or until onions are golden. Serve warm.   *Makes 6 side-dish servings*

Prep Time: 20 minutes
Cook Time: 25 minutes

Dijonnaise Potato Salad

1 cup HELLMANN'S® or BEST FOODS® Real or Light Mayonnaise or Low Fat Mayonnaise Dressing
2 tablespoons HELLMANN'S® or BEST FOODS® DIJONNAISE™ Creamy Mustard Blend
2 tablespoons chopped fresh dill *or* 1½ teaspoons dried dill weed
½ teaspoon salt
¼ teaspoon freshly ground pepper
1½ pounds small red potatoes, cooked and quartered
1 cup sliced radishes
½ cup chopped green onions

1. In large bowl, combine mayonnaise, creamy mustard blend, dill, salt and pepper.

2. Stir in potatoes, radishes and green onions.

3. Cover; chill.   *Makes about 8 servings*

Hot German Potato Salad

Gourmet Deli Potato & Pea Salad

1½ pounds new potatoes, scrubbed and quartered
1 cup water
¾ teaspoon salt, divided
½ pound sugar snap peas or snow peas, trimmed
⅓ cup reduced-fat mayonnaise
⅓ cup plain nonfat yogurt
⅓ cup finely chopped red onion
3 tablespoons FRENCH'S® Dijon Mustard
2 tablespoons minced fresh dill *or*
    2 teaspoons dried dill weed
1 clove garlic, minced

Microwave Directions: Place potatoes, water and ½ teaspoon salt in 3-quart microwave-safe baking dish. Cover and microwave on HIGH 15 minutes or until potatoes are tender, stirring once. Add peas. Cover and microwave on HIGH 3 minutes or until peas are crisp-tender. Rinse with cold water and drain. Cool completely.

Combine mayonnaise, yogurt, onion, mustard, dill, garlic and remaining ¼ teaspoon salt in large bowl; mix well. Add potatoes and peas; toss to coat evenly. Cover and refrigerate 1 hour before serving. Garnish as desired.

Makes 6 side-dish servings

Prep Time: 15 minutes
Cook Time: 18 minutes
Chill Time: 1 hour

Smoky Potato Salad

2 pounds new potatoes, peeled and quartered
¾ teaspoon salt
2 tablespoons vegetable oil
4 large green onions, cut into ½-inch pieces
2 cloves garlic, minced
1 teaspoon all-purpose flour
¼ teaspoon sugar
3 tablespoons FRANK'S® Original REDHOT® Cayenne Pepper Sauce
¼ teaspoon liquid smoke

1. Place potatoes, 1 cup water and salt in 3-quart microwavable baking dish. Cover; microwave on HIGH 15 minutes or until potatoes are fork-tender, stirring once. Rinse under cold water; drain.

2. Heat oil in 10-inch nonstick skillet over medium heat. Add onions and garlic; cook and stir 2 minutes or just until tender. Stir in flour and sugar; cook, stirring, 1 minute. Combine ½ cup water, RedHot® sauce and liquid smoke in small bowl. Gradually stir into onion mixture. Bring to a boil. Reduce heat; cook, stirring constantly, 1 to 2 minutes or until mixture thickens slightly.

3. Gently add potatoes to skillet, stirring until coated with dressing and heated through. Serve warm. *Makes 6 servings*

Note: This microwave method insures evenly cooked potatoes that do not fall apart. However, potatoes may be boiled in a saucepan on a conventional stove.

Gourmet Deli Potato & Pea Salad

Sweet Potato Salad

2 pounds sweet potatoes, peeled and cubed
2 tablespoons lemon juice
1 cup HELLMANN'S® or BEST FOODS®
  Real or Light Mayonnaise or Low Fat
  Mayonnaise Dressing
1 teaspoon grated orange peel
2 tablespoons orange juice
1 tablespoon honey
1 teaspoon chopped fresh ginger
¼ teaspoon salt
⅛ teaspoon nutmeg
1 cup coarsely chopped pecans
1 cup sliced celery
⅓ cup chopped pitted dates
  Lettuce leaves
1 can (11 ounces) mandarin orange
  sections, drained

1. In medium saucepan cook potatoes 8 to 10 minutes in boiling, salted water just until tender. (Do not overcook.) Drain. Toss with lemon juice.

2. In large bowl combine mayonnaise, orange peel, orange juice, honey, ginger, salt and nutmeg. Stir in warm potatoes, pecans, celery and dates. Cover; chill.

3. To serve, spoon salad onto lettuce-lined platter. Arrange orange sections around salad. Garnish as desired.   *Makes 6 servings*

Apple Pesto Potato Salad

  Pesto Sauce (recipe follows)
¾ cup cubed cooked boiling potatoes
¼ cup sliced radishes
¼ cup sliced olives
1 green onion, diagonally sliced
1 tablespoon olive oil
1 tablespoon white wine vinegar
½ teaspoon sugar
½ teaspoon grated lemon peel
¼ teaspoon salt
¼ teaspoon ground black pepper
2 Washington Golden Delicious apples,
  cored and thinly sliced

Prepare Pesto Sauce; set aside. Peel potatoes, if desired; slice. In large bowl, combine potatoes, radishes, olives and green onion. In small bowl, blend 2 tablespoons Pesto Sauce, olive oil, vinegar, sugar, lemon peel, salt and pepper; pour over potato mixture. Stir gently to coat. Marinate 1 to 2 hours. Arrange salad on serving plate with apple slices; serve.

Makes 4 servings

Pesto Sauce: In blender or food processor, combine ½ cup fresh basil leaves, ¼ cup grated Parmesan cheese, 2 tablespoons pine nuts, 1 tablespoon olive oil, 1 garlic clove and 1 teaspoon lemon juice; purée until smooth.

Favorite recipe from **Washington Apple Commission**

Sweet Potato Salad

Warm Tomato-Potato Salad

    3 medium (about 1 pound) tomatoes
    1 pound small red skinned potatoes,
        quartered
    3 slices bacon, cut into ½-inch pieces
    ¼ cup chopped onion
 1½ teaspoons sugar
    ½ teaspoon all-purpose flour
    1 teaspoon salt
    ⅛ teaspoon ground black pepper
    1 tablespoon cider vinegar
    ¼ cup water
    1 cup fresh or frozen sugar snap peas

Use tomatoes held at room temperature until fully ripe. Core tomatoes; cut into large chunks (makes about 3 cups). Set aside. In large saucepan cook potatoes in enough water to cover until tender, 10 to 15 minutes; drain. Set aside. Meanwhile, in large skillet cook bacon, stirring occasionally, until crisp, 3 to 5 minutes. Using a slotted spoon transfer bacon to paper towel to drain. Remove all but 1 tablespoon drippings from skillet; stir in onion. Cook, stirring occasionally, until tender, 5 to 7 minutes. Add sugar, flour, salt and pepper, stirring until smooth. Stir in vinegar, water and sugar snap peas; cook and stir until mixture boils and thickens slightly, 1 to 2 minutes. Stir in reserved potatoes and bacon. Add reserved tomatoes, tossing to coat. Place potato mixture on large serving plate.

Makes 6 servings (5 cups)

Favorite recipe from **Florida Tomato Committee**

Chicken Potato Salad Olé

    2 large ripe tomatoes, seeded and chopped
    ¾ cup chopped green onions
    ¼ cup fresh cilantro leaves, chopped
    1 to 2 tablespoons chopped, seeded, pickled
        jalapeño peppers
 1½ teaspoons salt, divided
    1 cup HELLMANN'S® or BEST FOODS®
        Real or Light Mayonnaise or Low Fat
        Mayonnaise Dressing
    3 tablespoons lime juice
    1 teaspoon chili powder
    1 teaspoon ground cumin
    2 pounds small red potatoes, cooked and
        sliced ¼ inch thick
    2 cups shredded cooked chicken
    1 large yellow or red bell pepper, diced
        Lettuce leaves
        Tortilla chips, lime slices, whole chili
        peppers and cilantro sprigs for garnish
        (optional)

1. In medium bowl, combine tomatoes, onions, chopped cilantro, jalapeño peppers and 1 teaspoon salt; set aside.

2. In large bowl, combine mayonnaise, lime juice, chili powder, cumin and remaining ½ teaspoon salt. Add potatoes, chicken, bell pepper and half of tomato mixture; toss to coat well. Cover; chill.

3. To serve, spoon salad onto lettuce-lined platter. Spoon remaining tomato mixture over salad. If desired, garnish with tortilla chips, lime slices, whole chili peppers and cilantro sprigs.

Makes 6 servings

Wisconsin True Blue Potato Salad

1¼ cups dairy sour cream
2 tablespoons minced parsley
2 tablespoons tarragon white wine vinegar
½ teaspoon celery seed
½ teaspoon salt
⅛ teaspoon black pepper
¾ cup (3 ounces) crumbled Wisconsin Blue cheese
4 cups cubed cooked potatoes
½ cup diced celery
½ cup green onion slices
½ cup sliced water chestnuts

Combine sour cream, parsley, vinegar, celery seed, salt and pepper; mix well. Stir in Blue cheese. Pour over combined potatoes, celery, onion and water chestnuts; toss lightly.

Makes 6 servings

Favorite recipe from **Wisconsin Milk Marketing Board**

Green Bean Potato Salad

1½ pounds slender green beans, ends trimmed and cut in half
6 small red potatoes, cubed
1 small red onion, thinly sliced lengthwise from stem to root
¼ cup WESSON® Canola Oil
¼ cup red wine vinegar
¼ cup seasoned rice vinegar
1 tablespoon garlic salt
1½ teaspoons seasoned pepper
1 teaspoon sugar

In large pot of boiling water, cook green beans about 7 minutes or until crisp-tender. Drain and immerse beans in ice water for 5 minutes to stop cooking process. Completely cool and drain well. In large pot of water, cook potatoes until tender. Repeat cooling procedure with potatoes. Place beans in large serving bowl. Add potatoes and onion. In small bowl, whisk together Wesson® Oil, vinegars, garlic salt, seasoned pepper and sugar. Pour dressing over vegetables; toss gently to coat. Cover and refrigerate 2 hours, tossing a few times during refrigeration. Remove salad from refrigerator a half hour before serving; toss just before serving.

Makes 6 servings

Ranch Picnic Potato Salad

6 medium potatoes (about 3½ pounds), cooked, peeled and sliced
½ cup chopped celery
¼ cup sliced green onions
2 tablespoons chopped parsley
1 teaspoon salt
⅛ teaspoon black pepper
1 tablespoon Dijon-style mustard
1 cup prepared HIDDEN VALLEY RANCH® Original Ranch® salad dressing
2 hard-cooked eggs, finely chopped
Paprika

In large bowl, combine potatoes, celery, onions, parsley, salt and pepper. In small bowl, stir mustard into salad dressing; pour over potato mixture and toss lightly. Cover and refrigerate several hours. Sprinkle with eggs and paprika.

Makes 8 servings

Colorado Potato & Prosciutto Salad

1¼ pounds round red-skin Colorado potatoes, unpeeled (about 4 potatoes)
½ pound green beans, trimmed and sliced into 2½-inch lengths
1½ cups cooked fresh or thawed frozen corn kernels
1 red or green bell pepper, cored, seeded and cut into slivers
6 ounces mozzarella cheese, cut into ½-inch cubes
3 ounces thinly sliced prosciutto or ham, torn into strips
3 green onions, sliced
⅓ cup olive oil
¼ cup lemon juice
2 tablespoons water
1 or 2 cloves garlic, minced
1 tablespoon chopped fresh thyme *or* 1½ teaspoons dried thyme leaves
Salt and black pepper

Cook potatoes until tender. Cool; cut into ½-inch-thick slices, then cut into quarters. Cook green beans until tender; cool. In large serving bowl, combine potatoes, beans, corn, bell pepper, cheese, prosciutto and green onions. In small bowl, whisk together oil, lemon juice, water, garlic and thyme. Season with salt and black pepper to taste. Pour dressing over potato mixture and toss to coat. Serve immediately or refrigerate.

Makes about 8 cups (6 to 8 servings)

Favorite recipe from **Colorado Potato Administrative Committee**

Oriental Potato Salad

1½ cups HELLMANN'S® or BEST FOODS® Real or Light Mayonnaise or Low Fat Mayonnaise Dressing
3 tablespoons vinegar
2 tablespoons sesame oil*
2 tablespoons soy sauce
2 teaspoons sugar
1 teaspoon grated fresh ginger
½ teaspoon salt
⅛ teaspoon hot pepper sauce
7 to 8 medium potatoes, peeled, cooked and sliced
1½ cups diagonally sliced celery
1 can (8 ounces) sliced water chestnuts, drained
6 green onions, thinly sliced
Lettuce leaves
2 tablespoons toasted sesame seeds

*Sesame oil is available in the imported (Oriental) section of the supermarket or in specialty food shops.

1. In large bowl combine mayonnaise, vinegar, sesame oil, soy sauce, sugar, ginger, salt and hot pepper sauce.

2. Add potatoes, celery, water chestnuts and green onions; toss to coat well. Cover; chill.

3. To serve, spoon salad over lettuce-lined platter. Sprinkle with sesame seeds.

Makes 8 servings

Colorado Potato & Prosciutto Salad

Classic Potato Salad

   1 cup HELLMANN'S® or BEST FOODS®
       Real or Light Mayonnaise or Low Fat
       Mayonnaise Dressing
   2 tablespoons vinegar
 1½ teaspoons salt
   1 teaspoon sugar
   ¼ teaspoon freshly ground pepper
   5 to 6 medium potatoes, peeled, cubed and
       cooked
   1 cup sliced celery
   ½ cup chopped onion
   2 hard-cooked eggs, diced

In large bowl combine mayonnaise, vinegar, salt, sugar and pepper. Add potatoes, celery, onion and eggs; toss to coat well. Cover; chill to blend flavors.   *Makes about 8 servings*

Curried Lamb Potato Salad

   1 cup bite-size strips cooked American lamb
 1½ pounds small round potatoes, scrubbed
   ¾ cup fresh peas, cooked or frozen peas,
       thawed
   ¾ cup thinly sliced carrots
   ⅓ cup finely chopped red onion*
   ⅓ cup plain nonfat yogurt
   ¼ cup reduced-calorie mayonnaise
   2 tablespoons chopped prepared chutney
   2 tablespoons curry powder
   2 to 3 tablespoons lime or lemon juice
       Salt and black pepper

*Finely chopped green onions can be substituted for red onion.

Cook potatoes in boiling salted water until tender; drain, cool and cut into quarters. Combine potatoes, lamb, peas, carrots and onion in medium bowl. Combine yogurt, mayonnaise, chutney, curry and lime juice in small bowl. Add yogurt mixture to potato mixture; toss until coated. Season to taste with salt and pepper.   *Makes 6 servings*

Favorite recipe from **American Lamb Council**

Smoked Turkey and Fresh Vegetable Salad

   ½ pound smoked turkey breast, cut into
       ½-inch cubes
   1 cup cubed red-skinned potato, steamed
   1 cup fresh broccoli florets
   ½ cup thinly sliced yellow squash
   ½ cup coarsely grated carrot
   ¼ cup thinly sliced red bell pepper
   ¼ cup green onion slices
   ⅓ cup reduced-calorie mayonnaise
   1 teaspoon Dijon mustard
   1 teaspoon lemon juice
   ½ teaspoon dill weed
   ¼ teaspoon dried parsley flakes
   ⅛ teaspoon garlic powder

Combine turkey, potato, broccoli, squash, carrot, pepper and onions in medium bowl. Combine mayonnaise and remaining ingredients in small bowl. Add mayonnaise mixture to turkey mixture; gently toss until turkey and vegetables are coated. Cover and chill at least 1 hour.
                              Makes 2 servings

Favorite recipe from **National Turkey Federation**

Curried Lamb Potato Salad

Farmers' Market Salad

DRESSING

½ cup chopped peperoncini
⅓ cup seasoned rice vinegar
3 tablespoons country Dijon mustard
2 tablespoons chopped fresh dill
1½ teaspoons sugar
1½ teaspoons garlic salt
1½ teaspoons fresh lemon juice
1½ teaspoons grated fresh lemon peel
½ teaspoon coarsely ground pepper
⅔ cup WESSON® Best Blend Oil

SALAD

1 pound baby red potatoes, unpeeled
1 pound baby asparagus
1 pound mixed salad greens or spinach
  leaves, washed and drained
1 basket cherry tomatoes, halved or baby
  teardrop yellow tomatoes
1 large orange bell pepper, thinly sliced
4 hard boiled eggs, quartered

DRESSING

In blender or food processor, add all dressing ingredients except Wesson® Oil. Pulse ingredients and slowly add Wesson® Oil until dressing is partially smooth; refrigerate.

SALAD

In saucepan of water, cook potatoes until tender. Drain potatoes; immerse in ice water for 5 minutes to stop cooking process. Cool completely; drain well. In large pot of boiling water, cook asparagus until crisp-tender. Repeat cooling procedure with asparagus.

In large bowl, toss salad greens with ⅓ dressing. Evenly divide salad greens among 4 plates. Arrange potatoes, asparagus, tomatoes, bell pepper and eggs in sections over salad greens. Drizzle half the remaining dressing over arranged vegetables and eggs. Serve salad with remaining dressing, if desired.   *Makes 4 servings*

Country-Style Potato Salad

2 pounds cooked red potatoes, peeled and
  diced
3 green onions, cut into ½-inch pieces
10 cherry tomatoes, halved
2 hard-cooked eggs, chopped
⅓ cup mayonnaise
⅓ cup GREY POUPON® Dijon or
  COUNTRY DIJON® Mustard
2 tablespoons red wine vinegar
½ teaspoon garlic powder
⅛ teaspoon ground black pepper

In large bowl, combine potatoes, green onions, tomatoes and eggs; set aside.

In small bowl, blend remaining ingredients; stir into potato mixture, tossing to coat well. Cover; chill at least 2 hours to blend flavors.
          Makes 6 (1¼-cup) servings

Farmers' Market Salad

Chicken Salad Niçoise

Nonstick cooking spray
1 pound chicken tenders
½ cup red onion wedges (about 1 small)
Fresh spinach leaves (optional)
2 cups whole green beans, cooked and
    chilled
2 cups cubed red potatoes, cooked and
    chilled
2 cups halved cherry tomatoes
1 can (15½ ounces) Great Northern beans,
    drained and rinsed
Herb and Mustard Dressing (recipe
    follows)

1. Spray medium nonstick skillet with cooking spray; heat over medium heat until hot. Add chicken; cook and stir 7 to 10 minutes or until chicken is browned and no longer pink in center. Cool slightly; refrigerate until chilled.

2. Spray small nonstick skillet with cooking spray; heat over medium heat until hot. Add onion; cook and stir over low heat about 15 minutes or until onion is caramelized. Cool to room temperature.

3. Place spinach, if desired, on plates. Top with chicken, onion, green beans, potatoes, tomatoes and Great Northern beans. Drizzle with Herb and Mustard Dressing. Serve immediately.

Makes 6 servings

Herb and Mustard Dressing

¼ cup water
3 tablespoons balsamic or cider vinegar
1½ tablespoons Dijon mustard
1 tablespoon olive oil
1 teaspoon dried basil leaves
1 teaspoon dried thyme leaves
1 teaspoon dried rosemary
1 small clove garlic, minced

1. In small jar with tight-fitting lid, combine all ingredients; shake well. Refrigerate until ready to use; shake before using. *Makes about ⅔ cup*

Mediterranean Montrachet® Salad

1 head Boston lettuce, washed, drained,
    dried and separated
10 new potatoes, quartered and grilled
3 cups blanched, young green beans
4 medium tomatoes, cut into eighths
1 red pepper, peeled, seeded and julienned
1 yellow pepper, peeled, seeded and
    julienned
1 cup vinaigrette dressing
3 tablespoons coarsely chopped fresh basil
2 packages (3.5 ounces each)
    MONTRACHET®, cut into 4 slices

Divide lettuce among 6 plates. Divide remaining vegetables among plates. Drizzle each plate with vinaigrette. Garnish with fresh basil and Montrachet® slices. Serve at room temperature.

Makes 6 servings

Chicken Salad Niçoise

SIDE DISHES

Potatoes au Gratin

1½ pounds small red potatoes
6 tablespoons margarine or butter, divided
3 tablespoons all-purpose flour
½ teaspoon salt
¼ teaspoon white pepper
1½ cups milk
1 cup (4 ounces) shredded Cheddar cheese
4 green onions, thinly sliced
¾ cup cracker crumbs

Preheat oven to 350°F. Spray 1-quart round casserole with nonstick cooking spray.

Place potatoes in 2-quart saucepan; add enough water to cover potatoes. Bring to a boil over high heat. Cook, uncovered, about 10 minutes or until partially done. Potatoes should still be firm in center. Drain and rinse in cold water until potatoes are cool. Drain and set aside.

Meanwhile, melt 4 tablespoons margarine in medium saucepan over medium heat. Add flour, salt and pepper, stirring until smooth. Gradually add milk, stirring constantly until sauce is thickened. Add cheese, stirring until melted.

Cut potatoes crosswise into ¼-inch-thick slices. Layer ⅓ of potatoes in prepared dish. Top with ⅓ of onions and ⅓ of cheese sauce. Repeat layers twice, ending with cheese sauce.

Melt remaining 2 tablespoons margarine. Combine cracker crumbs and margarine in small bowl. Sprinkle evenly over top of casserole.

Bake, uncovered, 35 to 40 minutes or until hot and bubbly and potatoes are tender.

Makes 4 to 6 servings

Potatoes au Gratin

Scalloped Potatoes

2 tablespoons margarine
3 tablespoons all-purpose flour
2½ cups skim milk
3 tablespoons grated Parmesan cheese
  Black pepper
2 pounds Idaho potatoes, peeled, thinly sliced
  Ground nutmeg
  Salt
½ cup (2 ounces) shredded reduced-fat Swiss cheese, divided
3 tablespoons thinly sliced chives, divided

1. Preheat oven to 350°F. Spray 2-quart glass casserole with nonstick cooking spray.

2. Melt margarine in medium saucepan; stir in flour and cook over medium-low heat 1 to 2 minutes, stirring constantly. Using wire whisk, gradually stir in milk; bring to a boil. Cook, whisking constantly, 1 to 2 minutes or until mixture thickens. Stir in Parmesan cheese; season to taste with pepper.

3. Layer ⅓ potatoes in bottom of prepared casserole. Sprinkle potatoes with nutmeg, salt, ⅓ Swiss cheese and 1 tablespoon chives. Spoon ⅓ margarine mixture over chives. Repeat layers, ending with margarine mixture.

4. Bake 1 hour and 15 minutes or until potatoes are fork-tender. Cool slightly before serving. Garnish with additional fresh chives, if desired.
Makes 8 servings

Potatoes Jarlsberg

8 medium new potatoes, peeled and quartered
2 medium turnips, peeled and cut into chunks
1 medium onion, finely chopped
¼ cup butter or margarine, softened
¼ cup chopped fresh parsley
1¼ cups (5 ounces) shredded JARLSBERG Cheese, divided
½ teaspoon salt
¼ teaspoon grated nutmeg
⅛ teaspoon black pepper

In large saucepan, cook potatoes in lightly salted water 10 minutes. Add turnips and onion; cook 15 minutes longer or until vegetables are tender. Drain well. Beat with electric mixer until smooth. Beat in butter and parsley. Add ¾ cup Jarlsberg, salt, nutmeg and pepper. Reserve 1 cup mixture.

Spread remaining potato mixture into buttered 1½-quart baking dish. Press reserved potato mixture through pastry bag with star tip around edge of casserole.

Bake at 350°F 40 minutes. Sprinkle remaining ½ cup Jarlsberg in center of casserole. Bake 5 minutes longer.
Makes 8 servings

Scalloped Potatoes

Classica™ Fontina Potato Surprise

2½ pounds potatoes
3 tablespoons butter or margarine, melted
¼ cup CLASSICA™ Grated Parmesan cheese
1 egg
1 egg white
⅛ teaspoon salt
⅛ teaspoon ground nutmeg
4 tablespoons fine dry bread crumbs, divided
8 ounces CLASSICA™ brand Fontina, cut into chunks
¼ cup freshly grated sharp provolone cheese
¼ pound GALBANI® Prosciutto di Parma, cut into small pieces
2 tablespoons butter, cut into small pieces

In large saucepan, cook potatoes in boiling water over medium-low heat until tender; drain. Cool slightly; peel and cut in half. Press potatoes through food mill or mash until smooth. Combine potatoes, melted butter, Classica™ grated Parmesan cheese, egg, egg white, salt and nutmeg in large bowl; mix until smooth. Set aside.

Sprinkle ½ of bread crumbs in well-buttered 9-inch-round baking dish. Tilt dish to coat. Spread about ½ of potato mixture on bottom and side of dish.

Combine Classica™ Fontina, provolone and Galbani® Prosciutto di Parma in small bowl. Sprinkle over potato mixture in dish.

Cover with remaining potato mixture; sprinkle with remaining bread crumbs. Dot with pieces of butter.

Bake in preheated 350°F oven 40 minutes or until thin crust forms. Let stand 5 minutes. Invert baking dish onto serving plate, tapping gently to remove. Serve immediately.

Makes 4 to 6 servings

Potato Gorgonzola Gratin

1 pound (2 medium-large) Colorado baking potatoes, unpeeled and very thinly sliced
Salt
Black pepper
Ground nutmeg
½ medium onion, thinly sliced
1 medium tart green apple, such as pippin or Granny Smith, or 1 medium pear, unpeeled, cored and very thinly sliced
1 cup low-fat milk or half-and-half
¾ cup (3 ounces) Gorgonzola or other blue cheese, crumbled
2 tablespoons freshly grated Parmesan cheese

Preheat oven to 400°F. In 8- or 9-inch square baking dish, arrange half the potatoes. Season generously with salt and pepper; sprinkle lightly with nutmeg. Top with onion and apple. Arrange remaining potatoes on top. Season again with salt and pepper; add milk. Cover dish with aluminum foil. Bake 30 to 40 minutes or until potatoes are tender. Remove foil; top with both cheeses. Bake, uncovered, 10 to 15 minutes or until top is lightly browned.

Makes 4 to 6 servings

Favorite recipe from **Colorado Potato Administrative Committee**

Potato Gorgonzola Gratin

Cauliflower and Potato Masala

8 ounces medium red skin potatoes
2 tablespoons vegetable oil
1 teaspoon minced garlic
1 teaspoon finely chopped fresh ginger
1 teaspoon salt
1 teaspoon cumin seeds
1 teaspoon ground coriander
1½ cups chopped tomatoes, fresh or canned
1 head cauliflower (about 1¼ pounds), cut into florets
½ teaspoon Garam Masala* (recipe follows)
2 tablespoons chopped cilantro

*Also available at specialty stores or Indian markets

1. Peel potatoes. Cut lengthwise into halves with chef's knife; cut each half lengthwise into 3 wedges.

2. Heat oil in large saucepan over medium-high heat. Add garlic, ginger, salt, cumin and coriander; cook and stir about 30 seconds or until fragrant.

3. Add tomatoes; cook and stir 1 minute. Add cauliflower and potatoes; mix well. Reduce heat to low; cover and cook about 30 minutes or until vegetables are tender.

4. Stir in Garam Masala; mix well. Pour into serving bowl; sprinkle with cilantro. Garnish as desired.   *Makes 6 servings*

Garam Masala

2 teaspoons cumin seeds
2 teaspoons whole black peppercorns
1½ teaspoons coriander seeds
1 teaspoon fennel seeds
¾ teaspoon whole cloves
½ teaspoon whole cardamom seeds, pods removed
1 cinnamon stick, broken

Preheat oven to 250°F. Combine spices on pizza pan; bake 30 minutes, stirring occasionally. Transfer spices to clean coffee or spice grinder or use mortar and pestle to pulverize.

Rustic Potatoes au Gratin

½ cup milk
1 can (10¾ ounces) condensed Cheddar cheese soup, undiluted
1 package (8 ounces) cream cheese
1 clove garlic, minced
¼ teaspoon ground nutmeg
⅛ teaspoon black pepper
2 pounds baking potatoes, cut into slices
1 small onion, thinly sliced

Slow Cooker Directions: Heat milk in small saucepan over medium heat until small bubbles form around edge of pan. Remove from heat. Add soup, cheese, garlic, nutmeg and pepper. Stir until smooth. Layer ¼ of potatoes and onion in bottom of slow cooker. Top with ¼ of soup mixture. Repeat layers 3 times. Cover and cook on LOW 6½ to 7 hours or until potatoes are tender and most of liquid is absorbed.

Makes 6 servings

Cauliflower and Potato Masala

Scalloped Potatoes Nokkelost

1 cup chopped leeks
¼ cup (½ stick) butter or margarine
¼ cup all-purpose flour
1½ teaspoons salt
⅛ teaspoon black pepper
2 cups milk
8 cups sliced red-skinned potatoes, unpeeled
2 cups shredded NOKKELOST Cheese
¾ cup bread crumbs
¼ cup melted butter or margarine

In saucepan, cook leeks in ¼ cup butter until tender. Stir in flour, salt and pepper. Gradually stir in milk. Cook, stirring constantly, until thickened. In 2-quart buttered baking dish, layer half of the potatoes, half of the leek sauce and half of the cheese. Repeat layers. Bake, covered, at 375°F for 45 minutes. Uncover. Blend bread crumbs and ¼ cup melted butter. Sprinkle around edge of casserole. Bake 15 minutes longer.

Makes 8 servings

Cheese & Bacon Potato Bake

1 (14¼-ounce) can COLLEGE INN®
   Chicken or Beef Broth
5 medium potatoes, peeled and thinly sliced
1 large onion, thinly sliced
6 slices bacon
3 tablespoons all-purpose flour
1 cup (4 ounces) shredded sharp Cheddar
   cheese

In medium saucepan, over medium-high heat, heat broth to a boil; reduce heat. Add potatoes and onion; cover and simmer 5 minutes. Drain, reserving 1½ cups broth. In medium skillet, over medium-high heat, cook bacon until crisp. Remove and crumble bacon; pour off all but 3 tablespoons drippings. Blend flour into reserved drippings. Gradually add reserved broth; cook and stir over medium heat until thickened. Stir in cheese until melted. In greased 2-quart baking dish, layer ⅓ each potato-onion mixture, sauce and bacon. Repeat layers twice. Bake at 400°F for 35 minutes or until potatoes are tender and sauce is bubbly.

Makes 6 servings

Tomato Scalloped Potatoes

1 can (14½ ounces) DEL MONTE®
   FreshCut™ Brand Diced Tomatoes
1 pound red potatoes, thinly sliced
1 medium onion, chopped
½ cup whipping cream
1 cup (4 ounces) shredded Swiss cheese
3 tablespoons grated Parmesan cheese

1. Preheat oven to 350°F.

2. Drain tomatoes, reserving liquid; pour liquid into measuring cup. Add water to measure 1 cup. Add reserved liquid, potatoes and onion to large skillet; cover. Cook 10 minutes or until tender.

3. Place potato mixture in 1-quart baking dish; top with tomatoes and cream. Sprinkle with cheeses.

4. Bake 20 minutes or until hot and bubbly. Sprinkle with chopped parsley, if desired.

Makes 6 servings

Rosy Potato and Pepper Gratin

3 tablespoons extra virgin olive oil
1 tablespoon fresh thyme leaves *or*
    1 teaspoon dried thyme
½ teaspoon salt
½ teaspoon freshly ground black pepper
3 pounds unpeeled red-skinned potatoes,
    sliced ¼ inch thick (4 cups)
2 cups thin strips yellow onion
2 cups thin strips red bell pepper
3 cups (12 ounces) shredded ALPINE
    LACE® Fat Free Pasteurized Process
    Skim Milk Cheese Product — For
    Mozzarella Lovers
¼ cup low sodium chicken broth
¼ cup white wine or chicken broth
    Sprigs of fresh thyme (optional)

1. Preheat the oven to 375°F. Spray a 13×9×3-inch baking dish with nonstick cooking spray. In a cup, mix the oil, thyme, salt and black pepper.

2. Half-fill a large saucepan with water and bring to a boil over high heat. Add the potatoes, cover, remove from the heat and let stand for 10 minutes. Drain the potatoes well and transfer them to a large bowl. Drizzle with the oil mixture.

3. Line the bottom of the baking dish with a third of the potatoes. Layer with half of the onions, half of the bell pepper strips and a third of the cheese. Repeat layers beginning with the potatoes, then top with the remaining third of the potatoes and cheese.

4. In a measuring cup, combine the chicken broth and wine. Pour evenly over the gratin. Cover with foil and bake for 20 minutes. Remove the foil and bake for 30 minutes or until the potatoes are tender and the top is golden brown. Garnish with the thyme sprigs, if you wish.   *Makes 8 servings*

Roasted Garlic Mashed Potatoes

1 large bulb garlic
    Olive oil
¼ cup chopped green onions
¼ cup margarine or butter
2½ pounds potatoes, peeled, cubed and
    cooked
1½ cups milk
½ cup GREY POUPON® Dijon Mustard
½ cup shredded Cheddar cheese (2 ounces)
¼ cup chopped parsley
    Salt and black pepper to taste

To roast garlic, peel off loose paperlike skin from bulb. Coat garlic bulb lightly with olive oil; wrap in foil. Place in small baking pan. Bake at 400°F for 40 to 45 minutes; cool. Separate cloves. Squeeze cloves to extract pulp; discard skins.

In large saucepan, over medium heat, sauté garlic pulp and green onions in margarine until tender. Add cooked potatoes, milk, mustard and cheese. Mash potato mixture until smooth and well blended. Stir in parsley; season with salt and pepper. Serve immediately.   *Makes 8 servings*

Country-Style Mashed Potatoes

4 pounds Yukon gold or Idaho potatoes,
    unpeeled and cut into 1-inch pieces
6 large cloves garlic, peeled
½ cup nonfat sour cream
½ cup skim milk, warmed
2 tablespoons margarine
2 tablespoons finely chopped fresh rosemary
    or 1 teaspoon dried rosemary
2 tablespoons finely chopped fresh thyme *or*
    ½ teaspoon dried thyme leaves
2 tablespoons finely chopped parsley

1. Place potatoes and garlic in medium saucepan; cover with water. Bring to a boil. Reduce heat and simmer, covered, about 15 minutes or until potatoes are fork-tender. Drain well.

2. Place potatoes and garlic in large bowl. Beat with electric mixer just until mashed. Beat in sour cream, milk and margarine until almost smooth. Mix in rosemary, thyme and parsley.
Makes 8 (¾-cup) servings

Cheesy Mashed Potatoes and Turnips

2 pounds all-purpose potatoes, peeled
1 pound turnips, peeled
¼ cup milk
½ cup shredded Cheddar cheese
¼ cup butter or margarine
1 teaspoon TABASCO® Pepper Sauce
½ teaspoon salt

In large saucepan over high heat, combine potatoes and turnips with enough water to cover. Bring to a boil and reduce heat to low; cover and simmer 25 to 30 minutes or until vegetables are tender. Drain. Return vegetables to saucepan; heat over high heat for a few seconds to eliminate any excess moisture, shaking saucepan to prevent sticking.

In small saucepan over medium heat, bring milk to a simmer. In large bowl, mash vegetables. Stir in warmed milk, cheese, butter, TABASCO® Sauce and salt.
Makes 8 servings

Note: Potatoes may be made up to 2 days in advance and reheated in microwave or double boiler above simmering water.

Golden Mashed Potatoes

2½ cups cubed cooked potatoes, mashed
3 tablespoons milk
2 tablespoons butter or margarine
1 tablespoon chopped fresh chives
½ pound VELVEETA® Pasteurized Process
    Cheese Spread, cubed, divided
¼ cup (1 ounce) KRAFT® 100% Grated
    Parmesan Cheese

• Combine potatoes, milk, butter and chives; beat until fluffy. Stir in half of the process cheese spread. Spoon into 1-quart casserole; sprinkle with Parmesan cheese. Bake at 350°F, 20 to 25 minutes or until thoroughly heated. Top with remaining process cheese spread; continue baking until process cheese spread begins to melt.
Makes 4 to 6 servings

Country-Style Mashed Potatoes

Golden Apples and Yams

2 large yams or sweet potatoes
2 Washington Golden Delicious apples,
   cored and sliced crosswise into rings
¼ cup firmly packed brown sugar
1 teaspoon cornstarch
⅛ teaspoon ground cloves
½ cup orange juice
2 tablespoons chopped pecans or walnuts

Heat oven to 400°F. Bake yams 50 minutes or until soft but still hold their shape. (This can also be done in microwave.) Let yams cool enough to handle. *Reduce oven to 350°F.*

Peel and slice yams crosswise. In shallow 1-quart baking dish, alternate apple rings and yam slices, overlapping edges slightly. In small saucepan, combine sugar, cornstarch and cloves; stir in orange juice and mix well. Heat orange juice mixture over medium heat, stirring, until thickened; pour over apples and yams. Sprinkle with nuts; bake 20 minutes or until apples and yams are tender. *Makes 6 servings*

Favorite recipe from **Washington Apple Commission**

Festive Sweet Potato Combo

2 cans (16 ounces each) sweet potatoes,
   drained
1⅓ cups (2.8-ounce can) FRENCH'S®
   French Fried Onions, divided
1 large apple, sliced into thin wedges,
   divided
2 cans (8 ounces each) crushed pineapple,
   undrained
3 tablespoons packed light brown sugar
¾ teaspoon ground cinnamon

Preheat oven to 375°F. Grease 2-quart shallow baking dish. Layer sweet potatoes, ⅔ cup French Fried Onions and half of the apple wedges in prepared baking dish.

Stir together pineapple with liquid, sugar and cinnamon in medium bowl. Spoon pineapple mixture over sweet potato mixture. Arrange remaining apple wedges over pineapple layer.

Cover; bake 35 minutes or until heated through. Uncover; sprinkle with remaining ⅔ cup onions. Bake 3 minutes or until onions are golden.
Makes 6 servings

Prep Time: 10 minutes
Cook Time: 38 minutes

Golden Apples and Yams

Sweet Potato Gratin

3 pounds sweet potatoes (about 5 large)
½ cup butter or margarine, divided
¼ cup plus 2 tablespoons packed light brown sugar, divided
2 eggs
⅔ cup orange juice
2 teaspoons ground cinnamon, divided
½ teaspoon salt
¼ teaspoon ground nutmeg
⅓ cup all-purpose flour
¼ cup uncooked old-fashioned oats
⅓ cup chopped pecans or walnuts

Bake sweet potatoes until tender in preheated 350°F oven 1 hour. Or, pierce sweet potatoes several times with table fork and place on microwavable plate. Microwave at HIGH 16 to 18 minutes, rotating and turning over sweet potatoes after 9 minutes. Let stand 5 minutes.

While sweet potatoes are hot, cut lengthwise into halves. Scrape hot pulp from skins into large bowl.

Beat ¼ cup butter and 2 tablespoons sugar into sweet potatoes with electric mixer at medium speed until butter is melted. Beat in eggs, orange juice, 1½ teaspoons cinnamon, salt and nutmeg, scraping down side of bowl once. Beat until smooth. Pour mixture into 1½-quart baking dish or gratin dish; smooth top.

For topping, combine flour, oats, remaining ¼ cup sugar and remaining ½ teaspoon cinnamon in medium bowl. Cut in remaining ¼ cup butter until mixture becomes coarse crumbs. Stir in pecans. Sprinkle topping evenly over sweet potatoes.*

Preheat oven to 350°F.

Bake 25 to 30 minutes or until sweet potatoes are heated through. For a crisper topping, broil 5 inches from heat 2 to 3 minutes or until golden brown. *Makes 6 to 8 servings*

*At this point, Sweet Potato Gratin may be covered and refrigerated up to 1 day. Let stand at room temperature 1 hour before baking.

Hot Sweet Potatoes

4 small (4 ounces each) sweet potatoes
2 tablespoons margarine or unsalted butter, softened
½ teaspoon TABASCO® Pepper Sauce
¼ teaspoon dried savory leaves, crushed

In large saucepan cover potatoes with water. Cover and cook over high heat 20 to 25 minutes or until potatoes are tender. Drain potatoes and cut in half lengthwise.

Preheat broiler. In small bowl, combine margarine and TABASCO® Sauce. Spread ¾ teaspoon margarine mixture over cut side of each potato half. Season each with pinch of savory. Place on foil-lined broiler pan and broil, watching carefully, about 5 minutes or until lightly browned. Serve hot. *Makes 4 servings*

Sweet Potato Soufflé

3 eggs, separated
¾ cup sugar
1¼ cups mashed sweet potatoes, fresh or
   canned
1 cup chopped walnuts, divided
Sugar
Whipped cream (optional)

Preheat oven to 350°F.

Beat egg yolks in large bowl until frothy.
Gradually add sugar; beat until lemon colored.
Add sweet potatoes and ½ of walnuts; beat until
blended.

Beat egg whites in separate bowl until stiff peaks
form; fold into sweet potato mixture. Turn into
buttered and lightly sugared soufflé dish. Sprinkle
remaining walnuts on top. Dust with sugar. Bake
15 minutes. Serve immediately with whipped
cream, if desired.   *Makes 6 servings*

Favorite recipe from **Walnut Marketing Board**

Cinnamon Apple Sweet Potatoes

4 medium sweet potatoes
1½ cups finely chopped apples
½ cup orange juice
¼ cup sugar
1½ teaspoons cornstarch
½ teaspoon ground cinnamon
½ teaspoon grated orange peel

Microwave Directions: Prick potatoes with fork.
Place on paper towels and microwave on HIGH
10 to 13 minutes or until tender, turning halfway
through cooking. Set aside. In microwavable
bowl, combine remaining ingredients. Cover and
cook on HIGH 3 minutes; stir. Cook uncovered
on HIGH 1½ to 2½ minutes or until sauce is
thickened. Slit sweet potatoes and spoon sauce
over each.   *Makes 4 servings*

Tip: Sauce can be made ahead and reheated.

Favorite recipe from **The Sugar Association, Inc.**

Sweet Potato Puffs

2 pounds sweet potatoes
⅓ cup orange juice
1 egg, beaten
1 tablespoon grated orange peel
½ teaspoon ground nutmeg
¼ cup chopped pecans

1. Peel and cut sweet potatoes into 1-inch pieces.
Place potatoes in medium saucepan. Add enough
water to cover; bring to a boil over medium-high
heat. Cook 10 to 15 minutes or until tender.
Drain potatoes and place in large bowl; mash
until smooth. Add orange juice, egg, orange peel
and nutmeg; mix well.

2. Preheat oven to 375°F. Spray baking sheet
with nonstick cooking spray. Spoon potato
mixture into 10 mounds on prepared baking
sheet. Sprinkle pecans on tops of mounds.

3. Bake 30 minutes or until centers are hot.
Garnish, if desired.   *Makes 10 servings*

Jamaican Grilled Sweet Potatoes

2 large (about 1½ pounds) sweet potatoes or yams
3 tablespoons packed brown sugar
2 tablespoons softened margarine, divided
1 teaspoon ground ginger
2 teaspoons dark rum
1 tablespoon chopped fresh cilantro

1. Pierce potatoes in several places with fork. Place on paper towel in microwave. Microwave at HIGH 5 to 6 minutes or until crisp-tender when tested with fork, rotating ¼ turn halfway through cooking. Let stand 10 minutes. Diagonally slice about ½ inch off ends of potatoes. Continue cutting potatoes diagonally into ¾-inch-thick slices.

2. Combine brown sugar, 1 tablespoon margarine and ginger in small bowl; mix well. Stir in rum, then cilantro; set aside.

3. Melt remaining 1 tablespoon margarine. With half of melted margarine, lightly brush one side of each potato slice. Grill slices margarine-side down on covered grill over medium coals 4 to 6 minutes or until grillmarked. Brush tops with remaining melted margarine; turn over and grill 3 to 5 minutes or until grillmarked. To serve, spoon rum mixture equally over potato slices.

Makes 6 servings

Sweet 'n' Sassy Potato Casserole

3 pounds sweet potatoes, peeled and cut into 1-inch pieces
3 Anjou pears or tart apples, peeled and cut into 1-inch pieces
½ cup packed light brown sugar
½ cup maple or pancake syrup
2 tablespoons FRANK'S® Original REDHOT® Cayenne Pepper Sauce
2 teaspoons ground cinnamon
¼ teaspoon ground allspice
2 tablespoons unsalted butter

1. Place sweet potatoes in large saucepan; cover with water. Bring to a boil. Cook 10 to 15 minutes or until tender. Drain. Place potatoes and pears in greased 3-quart baking dish.

2. Preheat oven to 400°F. Combine sugar, maple syrup, RedHot® sauce and spices in medium bowl. Pour over potatoes and pears. Dot with butter. Cover tightly.

3. Bake 30 to 35 minutes or until heated through and pears are tender. Baste mixture with sauce occasionally. Sprinkle with chopped toasted almonds, if desired. *Makes 8 servings*

Prep Time: 25 minutes
Cook Time: 30 minutes

Jamaican Grilled Sweet Potatoes

Sautéed Garlic Potatoes

2 pounds boiling potatoes, peeled and cut
    into 1-inch pieces
3 tablespoons FILIPPO BERIO® Olive Oil
6 cloves garlic, skins on
1 tablespoon lemon juice
1 tablespoon chopped fresh chives
1 tablespoon chopped fresh parsley
    Salt and freshly ground black pepper

Place potatoes in large colander; rinse under cold running water. Drain well; pat dry. In large nonstick skillet, heat olive oil over medium heat until hot. Add potatoes in a single layer. Cook, stirring and turning frequently, 10 minutes or until golden brown. Add garlic. Cover; reduce heat to low and cook very gently, shaking pan and stirring mixture occasionally, 15 to 20 minutes or until potatoes are tender when pierced with fork. Remove garlic; discard skins. In small bowl, crush garlic; stir in lemon juice. Add to potatoes; mix well. Cook 1 to 2 minutes or until heated through. Transfer to serving dish; sprinkle with chives and parsley. Season to taste with salt and pepper. *Makes 4 servings*

Double-Baked Potatoes

3 large Idaho potatoes
4 tablespoons skim milk, warmed
1 cup shredded Cheddar cheese
¾ cup corn
½ teaspoon chili powder
½ teaspoon dried oregano leaves
1 cup chopped onion
½ to 1 cup chopped poblano chili peppers
3 cloves garlic, minced
½ teaspoon salt
¼ teaspoon black pepper
3 tablespoons chopped cilantro

1. Preheat oven to 400°F. Scrub potatoes under running water with soft vegetable brush; rinse. Pierce each potato with fork. Wrap each potato in aluminum foil. Bake about 1 hour or until fork-tender. Remove potatoes; cool slightly. *Reduce oven temperature to 350°F.*

2. Cut potatoes in half lengthwise; scoop out inside being careful not to tear shells. Set shells aside. Beat potatoes in large bowl with electric mixer until coarsely mashed. Add milk; beat until smooth. Stir in cheese, corn, chili powder and oregano. Set aside.

3. Spray medium skillet with nonstick cooking spray. Add onion, poblano peppers and garlic; cook and stir 5 to 8 minutes or until tender. Stir in salt and pepper.

4. Spoon potato mixture into reserved potato shells. Sprinkle with onion mixture. Place stuffed potatoes in small baking pan. Bake 20 to 30 minutes or until heated through. Sprinkle with cilantro. *Makes 6 servings*

Sautéed Garlic Potatoes

Potato-Swiss Galette

2 tablespoons butter substitute
1 pound yellow onions, sliced ¼ inch thick
    (2 cups)
1 teaspoon minced garlic
2 pounds unpeeled small red-skinned
    potatoes, sliced ¼ inch thick (4 cups)
  Nonstick cooking spray
½ teaspoon salt
¼ teaspoon freshly ground black pepper
1 cup (4 ounces) shredded ALPINE LACE®
    Reduced Fat Swiss Cheese
¼ cup minced fresh parsley
½ teaspoon snipped fresh rosemary leaves *or*
    ¼ teaspoon dried rosemary

1. In large nonstick skillet, melt butter over medium-high heat. Add onions and garlic; sauté for 5 minutes or until softened. Spray both sides of potatoes with cooking spray; sprinkle with salt and pepper. Add potatoes to skillet with onion mixture. Sauté for 5 minutes or until golden brown on both sides. Cover; cook, stirring occasionally, for 10 minutes or until potatoes are tender.

2. In small bowl, toss the cheese with parsley and rosemary. Sprinkle over potatoes and toss gently just until cheese has melted.   *Makes 6 servings*

Honey Mustard Roasted Potatoes

¾ cup Honey Thyme Mustard (recipe
    follows)
4 large baking potatoes (about 2 pounds)
  Salt and black pepper

Prepare Honey Thyme Mustard. Preheat oven to 375°F. Peel potatoes and cut each into 6 to 8 pieces. Place in large saucepan; cover with salted water. Bring to a boil over high heat. Reduce heat to low. Simmer, covered, 12 to 15 minutes or until just tender. Drain; transfer to large bowl. Add Honey Thyme Mustard; toss until potatoes are evenly coated. Line baking sheet with foil; spray with nonstick cooking spray. Arrange potatoes on baking sheet. Bake 20 minutes or until potatoes begin to brown around edges. Season to taste with salt and pepper before serving.   *Makes 4 servings*

Honey Thyme Mustard

1 cup Dijon mustard
½ cup honey
1 teaspoon dried thyme leaves, crushed

Whisk together all ingredients in small bowl until well blended. Transfer mixture to airtight container and refrigerate until ready to use.
      Makes 1½ cups

Favorite recipe from **National Honey Board**

Potato-Swiss Galette

Grilled Cajun Potato Wedges

3 large russet potatoes, washed and scrubbed (do not peel) (about 2¼ pounds)
¼ cup olive oil
2 cloves garlic, minced
1 teaspoon salt
1 teaspoon paprika
½ teaspoon dried thyme leaves, crushed
½ teaspoon dried oregano leaves, crushed
¼ teaspoon black pepper
⅛ to ¼ teaspoon ground red pepper
2 cups mesquite chips

1. Prepare barbecue grill for direct cooking. Preheat oven to 425°F.

2. Cut potatoes in half lengthwise; then cut each half lengthwise into 4 wedges. Place potatoes in large bowl. Add oil and garlic; toss to coat well.

3. Combine salt, paprika, thyme, oregano, black pepper and ground red pepper in small bowl. Sprinkle over potatoes; toss to coat well. Place potato wedges in single layer in shallow roasting pan. (Reserve remaining oil mixture left in large bowl.) Bake 20 minutes.

4. Meanwhile, cover mesquite chips with cold water; soak 20 minutes. Drain mesquite chips; sprinkle over coals. Place potato wedges on their sides on grid. Grill potato wedges, on covered grill, over medium coals 15 to 20 minutes or until potatoes are browned and fork-tender, brushing with reserved oil mixture halfway through grilling time and turning once with tongs.   *Makes 4 to 6 servings*

Southern Smothered Potatoes

3 tablespoons Chef Paul Prudhomme's VEGETABLE MAGIC®, divided
1 teaspoon dried mustard
¼ teaspoon ground allspice
4 tablespoons unsalted butter
3 medium potatoes, peeled and cut into ⅛-inch-thick slices
3 cups sliced onions
1 cup chicken stock or chicken broth

Combine Vegetable Magic, mustard and allspice thoroughly in small bowl.

Melt butter in large heavy skillet over high heat. When butter starts to sizzle, add potatoes and 2 tablespoons Vegetable Magic mixture. Cover and cook 4 to 6 minutes over high heat or until potatoes start turning golden brown and sticking to bottom of skillet, scraping the crusty material from skillet occasionally. Add onions and remaining Vegetable Magic mixture. Cover and cook 6 to 8 minutes or until potatoes have golden brown crust. Add chicken stock and scrape bottom of skillet until clean. Cook, uncovered, until stock is completely absorbed by the potatoes, about 3 to 4 minutes. Remove from heat, cover and let sit 5 minutes before serving.
                Makes 6 servings

Grilled Cajun Potato Wedges

Santa Fe Potato Cakes

3 cups cooked instant mashed potato flakes
   or leftover unbuttered mashed potatoes
1 can (4 ounces) diced green chilies, drained
⅔ cup cornmeal, divided
3 green onions, sliced
⅓ cup (about 1½ ounces) shredded Cheddar
   cheese
2 eggs, beaten
2 tablespoons chopped fresh cilantro
1 teaspoon chili powder
½ teaspoon LAWRY'S® Seasoned Salt
½ teaspoon LAWRY'S® Seasoned Pepper
2 tablespoons olive oil, divided
   Salsa
   Dairy sour cream

In large bowl, combine potatoes, chilies, ½ cup cornmeal, onions, cheese, eggs, cilantro, chili powder, Seasoned Salt and Seasoned Pepper; shape into eight patties. Sprinkle both sides with remaining cornmeal; set aside. In large nonstick skillet, heat 1 tablespoon oil over medium heat. Add four patties; cook 5 to 7 minutes or until golden brown, turning once. Remove from skillet; keep warm. Repeat with remaining oil and patties. Garnish as desired.

Makes 4 servings

Serving Suggestion: Serve with salsa and sour cream.

Norse Skillet Potatoes

1½ pounds new potatoes, scrubbed
1½ teaspoons fresh rosemary leaves
⅓ cup olive oil
1 to 2 tablespoons dried mustard
½ teaspoon freshly ground black pepper
1 pound JARLSBERG or NOKKELOST
   cheese, grated

Slice potatoes wafer thin, using vegetable slicer or food processor, dropping them into cold water to avoid discoloration. Rub rosemary between fingers to break leaves and reserve.

Preheat oven to 425°F. Heat oil in 12-inch cast iron skillet. Add potatoes; cook over medium-high heat, shaking pan gently to toss but not break potatoes. When potatoes are slightly limp, sprinkle with rosemary, mustard to taste and pepper. Shake well to mix. Press with spatula. Cook until brown and crisp on bottom, lifting carefully to check.

Sprinkle with cheese. Immediately place skillet in oven. Bake 2 to 3 minutes until cheese starts to bubble and brown.   *Makes 8 to 10 servings*

Santa Fe Potato Cakes

Rosemary Hash Potatoes

  2 tablespoons olive oil
  1 clove garlic, minced
  2 teaspoons snipped fresh rosemary leaves
  1½ pounds red skin potatoes, unpeeled and
        cut into ½-inch cubes
  ½ teaspoon salt
  ½ teaspoon black pepper

Heat oil in large skillet over medium heat until
hot. Add garlic and snipped rosemary; cook and
stir 2 minutes. Add potatoes, salt and pepper.
Cook 5 minutes, stirring occasionally. Reduce
heat to medium-low; cook, uncovered, about 20
minutes or until potatoes are golden brown and
crisp, turning occasionally. Garnish with
rosemary sprig and tomato, if desired. Serve hot.
Refrigerate leftovers.

Makes 4 to 6 side-dish servings

Favorite recipe from **Bob Evans**®

Colorado Potato Devils

  4 Colorado baking potatoes
    Salt and black pepper
  8 teaspoons whole seed or grainy mustard
  6 ounces mushroom, pepper or regular Brie
        cheese
  2 tablespoons finely chopped chives or green
        onion tops

Heat oven to 400°F. Prick potatoes in 5 or 6
places with tines of a fork. Bake potatoes 50 to
60 minutes or until tender and skins are crisp.
Cut potatoes crosswise into 4 thick slices.

With melon baller or small spoon, scoop out a
little potato from the center. Season with salt and
pepper; spread each hallowed-out center with ½
teaspoon mustard. Cut up brie into 16 chunks;
place one piece in each center. Sprinkle with
chives. Place on baking sheets. Bake at 400°F 15
to 20 minutes or until cheese has melted and
browned in spots. *Makes 8 servings*

Favorite recipe from **Colorado Potato Administrative
Committee**

Saucy Skillet Potatoes

  1 tablespoon MAZOLA® Margarine
  1 cup chopped onion
  ½ cup HELLMANN'S® or BEST FOODS®
        Real or Light Mayonnaise or Low Fat
        Mayonnaise Dressing
  ⅓ cup cider vinegar
  1 tablespoon sugar
  1 teaspoon salt
  ¼ teaspoon freshly ground pepper
  4 medium potatoes, cooked, peeled and
        sliced
  1 tablespoon chopped parsley
  1 tablespoon crumbled cooked bacon

1. In large skillet, melt margarine over medium
heat. Add onion; cook 2 to 3 minutes or until
tender-crisp.

2. Stir in mayonnaise, vinegar, sugar, salt and
pepper. Add potatoes; cook, stirring constantly,
2 minutes or until hot (do not boil).

3. Sprinkle with parsley and bacon.

Makes 6 to 8 servings

Rosemary Hash Potatoes

Dilled New Potatoes and Peas

1 pound (6 to 8) small new potatoes,
    quartered
2 cups frozen peas
1 jar (12 ounces) HEINZ® HomeStyle
    Turkey Gravy
½ cup light dairy sour cream
1 teaspoon dried dill weed

Cook potatoes in 2-quart saucepan in lightly salted boiling water 10 to 15 minutes or until tender. Add peas; cook 1 minute. Drain well. Combine gravy, sour cream and dill; stir into vegetable mixture. Heat (do not boil), stirring occasionally.   *Makes 8 servings (about 4 cups)*

Three-Peppered Potatoes

1½ pounds medium potatoes, unpeeled, halved
    lengthwise
¼ cup olive or vegetable oil
1 *each* medium red, green and yellow bell
    pepper, thinly sliced
1½ teaspoons LAWRY'S® Seasoned Salt
¾ teaspoon dried oregano leaves, crushed
½ teaspoon LAWRY'S® Lemon Pepper
2½ tablespoons red wine vinegar

In large saucepan, cook potatoes in boiling water to cover 20 minutes or until tender. Drain and rinse under cold running water to cool. Cut each potato half into 3 wedges.

In large skillet, heat oil; cook bell peppers, Seasoned Salt, oregano and Lemon Pepper over medium-high heat 3 minutes or until tender. Add potatoes and vinegar; cook additional 3 to 5 minutes. Serve hot.   *Makes 6 servings*

Serving Suggestion: Serve with roast beef and a spinach and red onion salad.

Potatoes with Onions à la Smyrna

1 pound small red skin potatoes
⅓ cup FILIPPO BERIO® Olive Oil
1 large onion, thinly sliced
    Salt and freshly ground black pepper
1 tablespoon minced fresh Italian parsley

In medium saucepan, cook potatoes in boiling salted water 10 to 15 minutes or just until tender. Drain well; cool slightly. Cut potatoes into ½-inch slices. In large skillet, heat olive oil over medium-high heat until hot. Add onion; cook and stir 3 to 5 minutes or until limp but not brown. Gently add potato slices. Cook, stirring occasionally, 5 minutes or until heated through. Season to taste with salt and pepper; sprinkle with parsley.   *Makes 4 servings*

Flavorful SOUPS & STEWS

Vegetable Soup

2 tablespoons FILIPPO BERIO® Olive Oil
2 medium potatoes, peeled and quartered
2 medium onions, sliced
3 cups beef broth
8 ounces fresh green beans, trimmed and
    cut into 1-inch pieces
3 carrots, peeled and chopped
8 ounces fresh spinach, washed, drained,
    stems removed and chopped
1 green bell pepper, diced
2 tablespoons chopped fresh parsley
1 tablespoon chopped fresh basil *or*
    1 teaspoon dried basil leaves
½ teaspoon ground cumin
1 clove garlic, finely minced
Salt and freshly ground black pepper

In Dutch oven, heat olive oil over medium-high heat until hot. Add potatoes and onions; cook and stir 5 minutes. Add beef broth, green beans and carrots. Bring mixture to a boil. Cover; reduce heat to low and simmer 10 minutes, stirring occasionally.

Add spinach, bell pepper, parsley, basil, cumin and garlic. Cover; simmer an additional 15 to 20 minutes or until potatoes are tender. Season to taste with salt and black pepper. Serve hot.

Makes 6 to 8 servings

Spam™ Corn Chowder

1 cup chopped onion
1 tablespoon butter or margarine
1½ cups diced peeled potatoes
½ cup chopped green bell pepper
2 (17-ounce) cans cream-style corn
2 cups milk
1 (12-ounce) can SPAM® Luncheon Meat,
    cubed

In 3-quart saucepan over medium heat, sauté onion in butter 5 to 10 minutes or until golden. Add potatoes and bell pepper. Cook and stir 2 minutes. Add corn and milk. Bring to a boil. Reduce heat and simmer 15 minutes, stirring occasionally. Stir in Spam®. Simmer 2 minutes.

Makes 6 to 8 servings

Vegetable Soup

Creamy Shell Soup

4 cups water
3 or 4 chicken pieces
1 cup chopped onion
¼ cup chopped celery
¼ cup minced fresh parsley *or* 1 tablespoon
    dried parsley flakes
1 bay leaf
1 teaspoon salt
¼ teaspoon white pepper
2 medium potatoes, diced
4 or 5 green onions, chopped
3 chicken bouillon cubes
½ teaspoon seasoned salt
½ teaspoon poultry seasoning
4 cups milk
2 cups medium shell macaroni, cooked and
    drained
¼ cup butter or margarine
¼ cup all-purpose flour

Combine water, chicken, chopped onion, celery, minced parsley, bay leaf, salt and pepper in Dutch oven. Bring to a boil. Reduce heat to low; simmer until chicken is tender. Remove bay leaf; discard. Remove chicken; cool. Skin, debone and cut into small cubes; set aside.

Add potatoes, green onions, bouillon cubes, seasoned salt and poultry seasoning to broth. Simmer 15 minutes. Add milk, macaroni and chicken; return to simmer.

Melt butter in skillet over medium heat. Add flour, stirring constantly, until mixture begins to brown. Add to soup; blend well.

Let soup simmer on very low heat 20 minutes to blend flavors. Season to taste. Sprinkle with ground nutmeg and additional chopped parsley, if desired.   *Makes 8 servings*

Favorite recipe from **North Dakota Wheat Commission**

Vegetable and Shrimp Chowder

1½ cups diced Spanish onions
½ cup sliced carrots
½ cup diced celery
2 tablespoons margarine or butter
2 cups peeled and diced baking potatoes
1 (10-ounce) package frozen corn
5 cups COLLEGE INN® Chicken Broth or
    Lower Sodium Chicken Broth
½ pound small shrimp, peeled and deveined
⅓ cup GREY POUPON® Dijon Mustard
¼ cup chopped parsley

In large saucepan, over medium heat, cook onions, carrots and celery in margarine 3 to 4 minutes or until tender. Add potatoes, corn and chicken broth; heat to a boil. Reduce heat; simmer 20 to 25 minutes or until potatoes are tender. Add shrimp, mustard and parsley; cook 5 minutes more or until shrimp are cooked. Garnish as desired. Serve warm.
        Makes 8 servings

Vegetable and Shrimp Chowder

Fennel and Potato Bisque

⅔ pound fennel bulb with 1-inch stalk
3 tablespoons butter or margarine
1 leek, trimmed, washed
3 cups milk
1 tablespoon vegetable bouillon granules
½ teaspoon ground white pepper
2 cups cubed peeled red potatoes
1 cup half-and-half
3 tablespoons dry sherry
2 tablespoons all-purpose flour
4 ounces blue cheese, crumbled
¼ cup plus 2 tablespoons finely chopped
    toasted walnuts

1. To prepare fennel, wash fennel bulb. Trim stalks from top of bulb, reserving feathery leaves for garnish. Trim bottom of bulb leaving ⅛ inch of base. Remove any dry or discolored outer layers. Cut bulb into quarters; trim core from wedges. Cut into thin slices; cut slices crosswise in half.

2. Melt butter in large saucepan over medium heat. Add leek; cook and stir 10 minutes or until tender.

3. Add milk, bouillon granules and pepper. Bring to a boil over medium-high heat. Add fennel and potatoes. Reduce heat to low. Cover and simmer 15 to 20 minutes or until fennel is very tender.

4. Combine half-and-half, sherry and flour in small bowl; whisk until smooth.

5. Stir flour mixture into fennel mixture. Cook over medium heat until mixture thickens, stirring constantly. *Do not boil.*

6. Ladle soup into soup bowls; sprinkle each serving with one quarter of the blue cheese and 1½ tablespoons of the walnuts. Garnish, if desired. *Makes 4 servings*

Vichyssoise

4 medium leeks, sliced (white part only)
1 medium onion, sliced
¼ cup butter or margarine
2 pounds potatoes, peeled and thinly sliced
    (about 6 medium)
4 cups chicken broth
2½ cups milk
    Salt
2 cups half-and-half or light cream
    Chopped chives (optional)

Sauté leeks and onion in butter in large saucepan. Add potatoes and chicken broth. Bring to a boil. Reduce heat; simmer 30 minutes or until potatoes are very tender. Place potato mixture in food processor or blender container. Cover; process until smooth. Return mixture to saucepan. Add milk; season with salt. Bring mixture to a boil; remove from heat. Cool. Strain mixture through fine sieve. Add half-and-half to strained mixture; chill. Spoon soup into chilled bowls or cups. Sprinkle with chives, if desired. *Makes 8 to 10 servings*

Fennel and Potato Bisque

Sweet Potato and Ham Soup

1 tablespoon butter or margarine
1 small leek, sliced
1 clove garlic, minced
4 cups low-sodium chicken broth
2 medium sweet potatoes, peeled and cut
    into ¾-inch cubes
½ pound ham, cut into ½-inch cubes
½ teaspoon dried thyme leaves
2 ounces fresh spinach, rinsed, stemmed and
    coarsely chopped

Melt butter in large saucepan over medium heat.
Add leek and garlic. Cook and stir until leek is
tender.

Add chicken broth, sweet potatoes, ham and
thyme to saucepan. Bring to a boil over high
heat. Reduce heat to medium-low; cook 10
minutes or until sweet potatoes are tender.

Stir spinach into soup. Simmer, uncovered, 2
minutes more or until spinach is wilted. Serve
immediately.   *Makes 6 servings*

Chicken Pepper Pot Soup

2 tablespoons vegetable oil
2 large celery ribs, diced
1 large green bell pepper, diced
1 medium onion, diced
3 medium all-purpose potatoes, peeled and
    diced
3 tablespoons all-purpose flour
5 cups chicken broth
2 teaspoons TABASCO® Pepper Sauce
½ teaspoon dried thyme leaves
¼ teaspoon ground allspice
¼ teaspoon salt
½ pound boneless skinless chicken breast
    halves
¼ cup fresh chopped parsley

In 5-quart saucepan, heat oil over medium heat.
Add celery, bell pepper and onion; cook about 5
minutes. Add potatoes; cook 5 minutes longer,
stirring occasionally.

Stir flour into mixture; cook 1 minute. Add
chicken broth, TABASCO® Sauce, thyme,
allspice and salt. Over high heat, heat to boiling;
reduce heat to low. Cover and simmer 10
minutes.

Meanwhile, cut chicken breasts into bite-size
chunks; add to vegetable mixture in saucepan.
Cover and simmer 5 minutes longer or until
chicken and potatoes are tender. Stir in chopped
parsley.   *Makes 6 servings*

Sweet Potato and Ham Soup

Potato & Cheddar Soup

2 cups water
2 cups red potatoes, peeled and cubed
3 tablespoons butter or margarine
1 small onion, finely chopped
3 tablespoons all-purpose flour
    Red and black pepper to taste
3 cups milk
½ teaspoon sugar
1 cup (4 ounces) shredded Cheddar cheese
1 cup cubed cooked ham

Bring water to a boil in large saucepan. Add potatoes and cook until tender. Drain, reserving liquid. Measure 1 cup, adding water if necessary. Melt butter in saucepan over medium heat. Add onion; cook and stir until tender but not brown. Add flour; season with red and black pepper. Cook 3 to 4 minutes. Gradually add potatoes, reserved liquid, milk and sugar to onion mixture; stir well. Add cheese and ham. Simmer over low heat 30 minutes, stirring frequently.   *Makes 12 servings*

Creamy Asparagus Potato Soup

1 can (14½ ounces) DEL MONTE®
    FreshCut™ Brand Whole New
    Potatoes, drained
1 can (12 ounces) DEL MONTE®
    FreshCut™ Asparagus Spears, drained
½ teaspoon dried thyme, crushed
⅛ teaspoon garlic powder
1 can (14 ounces) chicken broth
1 cup milk or half-and-half

1. Place potatoes, asparagus, thyme and garlic powder in food processor or blender (in batches, if needed); process until smooth.

2. Pour into medium saucepan; add broth. Bring to a boil. Stir in milk; heat through. *(Do not boil.)* Season with salt and pepper to taste, if desired. Serve hot or cold. Thin with additional milk or water, if desired.   *Makes 4 servings*

Prep Time: 5 minutes
Cook Time: 5 minutes

Dilled Vichyssoise

1 cup chopped leeks
1 large potato, peeled and cubed
¼ cup finely chopped green onions
2 cloves garlic, minced
2 teaspoons sugar
3 cups chicken broth
1 cup water
¾ cup 2% milk
2 tablespoons fresh dill, chopped finely

Place leeks, potato, green onions, garlic and sugar in large saucepan. Add chicken broth and water; simmer over medium heat 15 to 20 minutes or until potatoes are very tender. Remove from heat; purée soup in food processor or blender in batches. Stir in milk and dill. Cover and refrigerate at least 3 hours before serving.   *Makes 6 servings*

Favorite recipe from **The Sugar Association, Inc.**

Potato & Cheddar Soup

Kaleidoscope Chowder

3 cups water
3 large potatoes, peeled and diced
1 (26-ounce) jar NEWMAN'S OWN®
    Diavolo Sauce
2 large carrots, peeled and thinly sliced
1½ to 2 pounds assorted seafood, such as fish
    fillets, bay scallops, shrimp or clams
½ cup dry white wine
2 cups shredded fresh spinach leaves
1 yellow bell pepper, seeded and diced
    Freshly grated Parmesan cheese

In large stockpot, bring water to a boil. Add potatoes; cook 5 minutes. Stir in Newman's Own® Diavolo Sauce and carrots. Bring to a boil; reduce heat and simmer 5 minutes.

Cut fish fillets into bite-size pieces. Peel and devein shrimp. Add seafood and wine to soup. Cook over medium-high heat, stirring often, until fish is opaque, 3 to 4 minutes. Add spinach and pepper; cover. Remove from heat and let stand until spinach and pepper are heated through, about 2 minutes. Serve with Parmesan cheese.   *Makes 4 servings*

Note: This chowder is also excellent with diced cooked chicken breast.

Seafood Bisque

2 leeks, cut in half lengthwise
2 tablespoons butter or margarine
3 cups milk
2 cups chopped peeled potatoes
1 (8-ounce) package imitation crab flakes,
    rinsed
½ teaspoon dried thyme leaves
⅛ to ¼ teaspoon hot pepper sauce
½ pound VELVEETA® Pasteurized Process
    Cheese Spread, cubed
2 tablespoons dry sherry (optional)

Thinly slice white portion and 1 inch of light green portion of leeks; sauté in butter.

Add all remaining ingredients except process cheese spread and sherry.

Bring to a boil. Reduce heat to low; cover. Simmer 15 minutes or until potatoes are tender.

Add process cheese spread and sherry; stir until process cheese spread is melted. Garnish with fresh chives and lemon peel.   *Makes 6 servings*

Kaleidoscope Chowder

Creamy Corn Bisque with Spicy Red Pepper Cream

RED PEPPER CREAM

1 jar (7 ounces) roasted red peppers,
    drained and patted dry
3 tablespoons sour cream
2 tablespoons FRANK'S® Original
    REDHOT® Cayenne Pepper Sauce

CORN BISQUE

1 tablespoon olive oil
1 large leek (white portion only), well
    rinsed and chopped* (1½ cups)
2 carrots, diced
¾ teaspoon dried thyme leaves
½ teaspoon dried basil leaves
1 can (14½ ounces) reduced-sodium
    chicken broth
¾ pound potatoes, peeled and cut into
    ½-inch pieces (2 cups)
1 can (10¾ ounces) condensed cream of
    corn soup
1 cup half-and-half
1 cup frozen corn
¼ teaspoon salt
1 tablespoon FRANK'S® Original
    REDHOT® Cayenne Pepper Sauce

*You may substitute 6 small green onions (white portion
only), chopped.

1. Combine roasted peppers, sour cream and 2 tablespoons RedHot® sauce in blender or food processor. Cover; process until puréed. Set aside.

2. Heat oil in large saucepan. Add leek and carrots; cook over medium heat 4 minutes or until just tender. Add thyme and basil; cook 1 minute. Stir in chicken broth and potatoes. Bring to a boil. Reduce heat to low; cook, covered, 5 minutes or until potatoes are just tender. Stir in corn soup, 1 cup water, half-and-half, corn and salt. Bring just to a boil. Reduce heat to low; cook 3 minutes, stirring. Stir in 1 tablespoon RedHot® sauce.

3. Ladle soup into bowls. Top with dollop of reserved red pepper cream; swirl into soup. Garnish with chives, if desired.

*Makes 6 servings
(7 cups soup, 1 cup pepper cream)*

Prep Time: 30 minutes
Cook Time: about 15 minutes

*Creamy Corn Bisque with Spicy Red
Pepper Cream*

Vegetable-Bean Chowder

½ cup chopped onion
½ cup chopped celery
2 cups water
½ teaspoon salt
2 cups cubed peeled potatoes
1 cup carrot slices
1 can (15 ounces) cream-style corn
1 can (15 ounces) cannellini beans, drained
    and rinsed
¼ teaspoon dried tarragon leaves
¼ teaspoon ground black pepper
2 cups low-fat (1%) milk
2 tablespoons cornstarch

1. Spray 4-quart Dutch oven or large saucepan with nonstick cooking spray; heat over medium heat until hot. Add onion and celery. Cook and stir 3 minutes or until crisp-tender.

2. Add water and salt. Bring to a boil over high heat. Add potatoes and carrot. Reduce heat to medium-low. Simmer, covered, 10 minutes or until potatoes and carrot are tender. Stir in corn, beans, tarragon and pepper. Simmer, covered, 10 minutes or until heated through.

3. Stir milk into cornstarch in medium bowl until smooth. Stir into vegetable mixture. Simmer, uncovered, until thickened. Garnish as desired. *Makes 5 (1½-cup) servings*

Potato-Cheese Calico Soup

1 pound potatoes, peeled and thinly sliced
1 cup sliced onion
2½ cups chicken broth
1 cup sliced mushrooms
½ cup diced red bell pepper
½ cup sliced green onions
½ cup low-fat milk
1 cup (4 ounces) finely shredded Wisconsin
    Asiago Cheese
Salt and black pepper (optional)
2 tablespoons chopped fresh parsley

In 3-quart saucepan, combine potatoes, 1 cup onion and broth. Bring to a boil. Reduce heat to low. Cover; cook until potatoes are tender, about 10 minutes. Transfer to blender container; blend until smooth. Return to saucepan. Stir in mushrooms, bell pepper, green onions and milk. Bring to a simmer over medium-low heat. Add cheese, a few tablespoons at a time, stirring to melt. Season with salt and black pepper. Sprinkle with parsley. *Makes 6 servings, 6 cups*

Favorite recipe from **Wisconsin Milk Marketing Board**

Vegetable-Bean Chowder

Corn and Onion Chowder

¼ pound uncooked bacon, chopped
2 medium potatoes (¾ pound), peeled and
     cut into ¼-inch cubes
1⅓ cups (2.8-ounce can) FRENCH'S®
     French Fried Onions, divided
½ cup chopped celery
1 tablespoon fresh thyme *or* ¾ teaspoon
     dried thyme leaves
1 bay leaf
1½ cups water
2 cans (15 ounces each) cream-style corn,
     undrained
1½ cups milk
½ teaspoon salt
¼ teaspoon ground white or black pepper

Cook and stir bacon in large saucepan over
medium-high heat until crisp and browned.
Remove with slotted spoon to paper towel. Pour
off all but 1 tablespoon drippings.

Add potatoes, ⅔ cup French Fried Onions,
celery, thyme and bay leaf to saucepan. Stir in
water. Bring to a boil over medium-high heat.
Reduce heat to low. Cover; simmer 10 to 12
minutes or until potatoes are fork-tender, stirring
occasionally.

Stir in corn, milk, salt, pepper and reserved
bacon. Cook until heated through. *Do not boil.*
Discard bay leaf. Ladle into individual soup
bowls. Sprinkle with remaining ⅔ cup onions.
Makes 6 to 8 servings

Prep Time: 20 minutes
Cook Time: 20 minutes

Cider Stew

2 pounds stew beef, cut into 1-inch cubes
2 tablespoons margarine
¼ cup all-purpose flour
2 cups water
1 cup apple cider
½ cup A.1.® Steak Sauce
2 teaspoons dried thyme leaves
½ teaspoon ground black pepper
1 bay leaf
3 medium potatoes, peeled and cut into
     1-inch cubes
3 medium carrots, sliced
1 medium onion, chopped
1 (10-ounce) package frozen cut green
     beans

In large heavy saucepan, over medium-high heat,
brown beef in margarine. Stir in flour. Gradually
stir in water, cider and steak sauce. Bring to a
boil over high heat; stir in thyme, pepper and
bay leaf. Reduce heat to low; cover and simmer 2
hours.

Add potatoes, carrots, onion and beans. Cover
and cook 30 minutes or until vegetables are
tender. Discard bay leaf before serving.
Makes 6 to 8 servings

French Beef Stew

1½ pounds stew beef, cut into 1-inch cubes
¼ cup all-purpose flour
2 tablespoons vegetable oil
2 cans (14½ ounces each) DEL MONTE®
  FreshCut™ Brand Diced Tomatoes
  with Garlic & Onion
1 can (14 ounces) beef broth
4 medium carrots, peeled and cut into
  1-inch chunks
2 medium potatoes, peeled and cut into
  1-inch chunks
¾ teaspoon dried thyme, crushed
2 tablespoons Dijon mustard (optional)

1. Combine meat and flour in large plastic food storage bag; toss to coat evenly.

2. Brown meat in hot oil in 6-quart saucepan. Season with salt and pepper, if desired.

3. Add all remaining ingredients except mustard. Bring to a boil; reduce heat to medium-low. Cover; simmer 1 hour or until beef is tender.

4. Blend in mustard. Garnish and serve with warm crusty French bread, if desired.

Makes 6 to 8 servings

Prep Time: 10 minutes
Cook Time: 1 hour

Pecos "Red" Stew

2 pounds boneless pork shoulder or sirloin,
  cut into 1½-inch cubes
2 tablespoons vegetable oil
2 cups chopped onions
1 cup chopped green bell pepper
¼ cup chopped fresh cilantro
2 cloves garlic, minced
3 to 4 tablespoons chili powder
2 teaspoons dried oregano leaves
1 teaspoon salt
½ teaspoon crushed red pepper
2 cans (14½ ounces each) chicken broth
3 cups cubed, peeled potatoes, cut into
  1-inch pieces
2 cups fresh or frozen whole kernel corn
1 can (16 ounces) garbanzo beans, drained

Heat oil in Dutch oven. Brown pork over medium-high heat. Stir in onions, bell pepper, cilantro, garlic, chili powder, oregano, salt, red pepper and chicken broth. Cover; cook over medium-low heat 45 to 55 minutes or until pork is tender. Add potatoes, corn and beans. Cover; cook 15 to 20 minutes longer.

Makes 8 servings

Prep Time: 20 minutes
Cook Time: 60 minutes

Favorite recipe from **National Pork Producers Council**

Spicy African Chick-Pea and Sweet Potato Stew

Spice Paste (recipe follows)
1½ pounds sweet potatoes, peeled and cubed
2 cups vegetable broth or water
1 can (16 ounces) plum tomatoes, undrained, chopped
1 can (16 ounces) chick-peas, drained and rinsed
1½ cups sliced fresh okra *or* 1 package (10 ounces) frozen cut okra, thawed
Yellow Couscous (recipe follows)
Hot pepper sauce
Fresh cilantro for garnish

1. Prepare Spice Paste.

2. Combine sweet potatoes, vegetable broth, tomatoes and juice, chick-peas, okra and Spice Paste in large saucepan. Bring to a boil over high heat. Reduce heat to low. Cover and simmer 15 minutes. Uncover; simmer 10 minutes or until vegetables are tender.

3. Meanwhile, prepare Yellow Couscous.

4. Serve stew with couscous and hot pepper sauce. Garnish, if desired.   *Makes 4 servings*

Spice Paste

6 cloves garlic, peeled
1 teaspoon coarse salt
2 teaspoons sweet paprika
1½ teaspoons cumin seeds
1 teaspoon cracked black pepper
½ teaspoon ground ginger
½ teaspoon ground allspice
1 tablespoon olive oil

Process garlic and salt in blender or small food processor until garlic is finely chopped. Add remaining spices. Process 15 seconds. While blender is running, pour oil through cover opening; process until mixture forms paste.

Yellow Couscous

5 green onions
1 tablespoon olive oil
1⅔ cups water
¼ teaspoon salt
⅛ teaspoon saffron threads *or* ½ teaspoon ground turmeric
1 cup precooked couscous*

*Check ingredient label for "precooked semolina."

1. Trim roots from onions; discard. Cut onions into slices.

2. Heat oil in medium saucepan over medium heat until hot. Add onions; cook and stir 4 minutes. Add water, salt and saffron. Bring to a boil. Stir in couscous. Remove from heat. Cover; let stand 5 minutes.   *Makes 3 cups*

Spicy African Chick-Pea and Sweet Potato Stew

Caribbean Turkey Stew

2 pounds turkey thighs, skin removed
1 tablespoon vegetable oil
3 cups thinly sliced onions
1½ pounds butternut squash, peeled, seeded and cut into 1-inch cubes
1 pound sweet potatoes, peeled and cut into 1-inch cubes
1 can (16 ounces) stewed tomatoes
1 cup canned reduced-sodium chicken broth or homemade turkey broth
¼ cup sweetened flaked coconut
½ teaspoon salt
½ teaspoon red pepper flakes
1 can (16 ounces) black beans,* drained

CONDIMENTS
2 medium bananas, sliced
1 bunch green onions, sliced
½ cup sweetened flaked coconut
1 to 2 limes, cut into wedges

*If canned black beans are unavailable, soak 8 ounces of dried black beans according to package directions. Add beans in step 2 with vegetables and turkey.

1. Brown turkey in oil in 5-quart Dutch oven over medium-high heat, about 3 minutes per side. Remove and set aside.

2. Add onions; cook and stir 2 to 3 minutes or until translucent. Add turkey, squash, sweet potatoes, tomatoes, broth, ¼ cup coconut, salt and red pepper. Bring to a boil. Reduce heat to low. Cover and simmer 1¼ to 1½ hours or until turkey thighs register 180° to 185°F in thickest portion.

3. Remove turkey thighs from stew and strip meat from bones; discard bones. Return turkey strips to stew and stir in beans. Cook until heated through.

4. To serve, spoon stew into bowls and serve with bananas, green onions and coconut. Squeeze lime juice over top.   *Makes 6 servings*

Favorite recipe from **National Turkey Federation**

Country Chicken Stew

2 tablespoons butter or margarine
1 pound boneless skinless chicken breasts, cut into 1-inch cubes
½ pound small red potatoes, cut into ½-inch cubes
2 tablespoons cooking sherry
2 jars (12 ounces each) golden chicken gravy
1 bag (16 ounces) BIRDS EYE® frozen Farm Fresh Mixtures Broccoli, Green Beans, Pearl Onions and Red Peppers
½ cup water

• Melt butter in large saucepan over high heat. Add chicken and potatoes; cook about 8 minutes or until browned, stirring frequently.

• Add sherry; cook until evaporated. Add gravy, vegetables and water.

• Bring to a boil; reduce heat to medium-low. Cover and cook 5 minutes.
                                Makes 4 to 6 servings

Country Chicken Stew

Brunswick Stew

1 stewing chicken, cut into serving pieces
   (about 4½ pounds)
2 quarts water
1 rib celery (including leaves), cut into
   2-inch pieces
1 small onion, quartered
1 small clove garlic, halved
2 teaspoons salt
1 teaspoon whole peppercorns
1 can (14½ ounces) tomatoes, cut into
   1-inch pieces
2 medium potatoes, pared and cubed
1 onion, thinly sliced
¼ cup tomato paste
1 teaspoon sugar
½ teaspoon ground black pepper
½ teaspoon dried thyme leaves
⅛ teaspoon garlic powder
   Dash red pepper sauce
1 package (10 ounces) frozen lima beans
1 package (10 ounces) frozen corn

Place chicken, giblets and neck in 5-quart Dutch oven; add water. Heat to boiling; skim off foam. Add celery, quartered onion, garlic, salt and peppercorns; heat to boiling. Reduce heat. Cover; simmer until thighs are tender, 2½ to 3 hours.

Remove chicken pieces from broth; cool slightly. Remove meat from chicken, discarding bones and skin. Cut enough chicken into 1-inch pieces to measure 3 cups. (Reserve remaining chicken for another use.)

Strain broth through double thickness of cheesecloth, discarding vegetables; skim off fat.

Return 1 quart broth to Dutch oven. (Reserve remaining broth for another use.) Add tomatoes, potatoes, sliced onion, tomato paste, sugar, ground pepper, thyme, garlic powder and red pepper sauce. Cook until boiling; reduce heat. Cover; simmer 30 minutes. Add beans and corn to stew. Cook until stew boils. Reduce heat. Cover; cook 5 minutes. Add chicken pieces; cook 5 minutes. Serve hot.   *Makes 6 to 8 servings*

Sweet Potato Cranberry Stew

2 teaspoons vegetable oil
1 pound lean pork, cut into 1-inch strips
1 tablespoon brown sugar
2 sweet potatoes, peeled and cut into
   chunks
½ teaspoon ground allspice
¼ teaspoon black pepper
¾ cup canned chicken broth*
2 cups cranberries

*One bouillon cube dissolved in ¾ cup water can be substituted for canned chicken broth.

Heat oil in medium saucepan over medium heat until hot. Add pork and sugar. Cook and stir 10 minutes or until lightly browned. Remove pork and set aside. Add sweet potatoes, allspice, pepper and broth. Simmer, covered, over low heat 15 minutes. Add cranberries and pork; simmer, covered, 15 minutes or until pork is tender.   *Makes 4 servings*

Favorite recipe from **The Sugar Association, Inc.**

Brunswick Stew

Jamaican Black Bean Stew

2 cups uncooked brown rice
2 pounds sweet potatoes
3 pounds butternut squash
1 can (about 14 ounces) vegetable broth
1 large onion, coarsely chopped
3 cloves garlic, minced
1 tablespoon curry powder
1½ teaspoons allspice
½ teaspoon ground red pepper
¼ teaspoon salt
2 cans (15 ounces each) black beans, drained and rinsed
½ cup raisins
3 tablespoons fresh lime juice
1 cup diced tomato
1 cup diced peeled cucumber

1. Prepare rice according to package directions. Peel sweet potatoes; cut into ¾-inch chunks to measure 4 cups. Peel squash; remove seeds. Cut into ¾-inch cubes to measure 5 cups.

2. Combine potatoes, squash, vegetable broth, onion, garlic, curry powder, allspice, pepper and salt in Dutch oven. Bring to a boil; reduce heat to low. Simmer, covered, 5 minutes. Add beans and raisins. Simmer 5 minutes or just until sweet potatoes and squash are tender and beans are hot. Remove from heat; stir in lime juice.

3. Serve stew over brown rice; top with tomato and cucumber. Garnish with lime peel.

Makes 8 servings

Home-Style Chicken and Sweet Potato Stew

4 boneless, skinless chicken breasts
Garlic salt and pepper
½ cup all-purpose flour
¼ cup WESSON® Vegetable Oil
2 cups cubed, peeled sweet potatoes
1 cup chopped onion
1 (14.5-ounce) can HUNT'S® Stewed Tomatoes, lightly crushed
¾ cup homemade chicken stock or canned chicken broth
¾ cup apple cider
½ teaspoon dried dill weed
1 cube chicken bouillon
Dash or two of GEBHARDT® Hot Pepper Sauce
Salt to taste

Rinse chicken and pat dry; cut into ½-inch pieces. Sprinkle with garlic salt and pepper. Place flour in plastic bag. Add chicken; shake until chicken is well coated. In large stockpot, heat Wesson® Oil. Add chicken; cook on both sides until golden brown. Remove chicken; set aside. In same pot, add sweet potatoes and onion; sauté until onion is tender. Stir in remaining ingredients except salt; blend well. Add browned chicken; bring to a boil. Reduce heat; cover and simmer 25 to 30 minutes or until chicken is no longer pink in center and potatoes are tender, stirring often. Salt to taste. *Makes 4 servings*

Hint: For a sweeter stew, substitute yams for sweet potatoes.

Jamaican Black Bean Stew

Hearty Sausage Stew

¼ cup olive oil
4 carrots, chopped
1 onion, cut into quarters
1 cup chopped celery
2 cloves garlic, finely chopped
1 teaspoon finely chopped fennel
   Salt and black pepper to taste
12 small new potatoes
1 pound mushrooms, cut into halves
2 cans (12 ounces each) diced tomatoes,
   undrained
1 can (8 ounces) tomato sauce
1 tablespoon dried oregano leaves
1 pound HILLSHIRE FARM® Polska
   Kielbasa,* sliced

*Or use any variety Hillshire Farm® Smoked Sausage.

Heat oil in heavy skillet over medium-high heat; add carrots, onion, celery, garlic, fennel, salt and pepper. Sauté until vegetables are soft. Add potatoes, mushrooms, tomatoes with liquid, tomato sauce and oregano; cook 20 minutes over low heat. Add Polska Kielbasa; simmer 15 minutes or until heated through.

Makes 6 servings

Arizona Turkey Stew

3 tablespoons olive oil or vegetable oil
5 medium carrots, cut into thick slices
1 large onion, cut into ½-inch pieces
1 pound sliced turkey breast, cut into
   1-inch strips
1 teaspoon LAWRY'S® Garlic Powder with
   Parsley
3 tablespoons all-purpose flour
8 small red potatoes, cut into ½-inch cubes
1 package (10 ounces) frozen peas, thawed
8 ounces sliced fresh mushrooms
1 cup beef broth
1 can (8 ounces) tomato sauce
1 package (1.62 ounces) LAWRY'S® Spices
   & Seasonings for Chili

In large skillet, heat oil; cook carrots and onion over medium heat until tender. Stir in turkey strips and Garlic Powder with Parsley; cook additional 3 to 5 minutes or until turkey is just browned. Stir in flour. Pour mixture into 3-quart casserole dish. Stir in remaining ingredients. Bake, covered, in 450°F oven 40 to 45 minutes or until potatoes are tender and turkey is no longer pink in center. Let stand 5 minutes before serving. *Makes 8 to 10 servings*

Serving Suggestion: Serve with warmed flour tortillas.

Hint: To prepare on the stovetop use a Dutch oven. Bring mixture to a boil over medium-high heat; reduce heat to low; cover and cook 40 to 45 minutes or until potatoes are tender and turkey is no longer pink in center. Let stand 5 minutes before serving.

Hearty Sausage Stew

ACKNOWLEDGMENTS

The publisher would like to thank the companies and organizations listed below for the use of their recipes and photographs in this publication.

Alpine Lace Brands, Inc.

American Lamb Council

A.1.® Steak Sauce

BC-USA, Inc.

Best Foods

Birds Eye®

Bob Evans®

Chef Paul Prudhomme's Magic Seasoning Blends®

COLLEGE INN® Broth

Colorado Potato Administrative Committee

Cucina Classica Italiana, Inc.

Delmarva Poultry Industry, Inc.

Del Monte Corporation

EGG BEATERS® Healthy Real Egg Substitute

Filippo Berio Olive Oil

The Fillo Factory

Florida Tomato Committee

GREY POUPON® Mustard

Guiltless Gourmet®

Healthy Choice®

Heinz U.S.A.

Hillshire Farm®

Hormel Foods Corporation

Hunt-Wesson, Inc.

The HV Company

Kellogg Company

Kraft Foods, Inc.

Lawry's® Foods, Inc.

McIlhenny Company (Tabasco® Pepper Sauce)

Michigan Apple Committee

MOTT'S® Inc., a division of Cadbury Beverages Inc.

National Foods

National Honey Board

National Pork Producers Council

National Turkey Federation

Newman's Own, Inc.®

Norseland, Inc.

North Dakota Wheat Commission

The Procter & Gamble Company

Reckitt & Colman Inc.

StarKist® Seafood Company

The Sugar Association, Inc.

Sunkist Growers

Walnut Marketing Board

Washington Apple Commission

Wisconsin Milk Marketing Board

INDEX

A

Apples, Cider and Applesauce
Apple Pesto Potato Salad, 112
Apple-Potato Pancakes, 34
Baked Apple & Sweet Potato
    Casserole, 52
Cider Stew, 172
Cinnamon Applesauce, 37
Cinnamon Apple Sweet Potatoes,
    140
Country Kielbasa Kabobs, 92
Festive Sweet Potato Combo, 136
German-Style Bratwurst &
    Sauerkraut, 94
Golden Apples and Yams, 136
Kielbasa Kabobs, 94
Latkes (Potato Pancakes), 36
Pork and Cabbage Ragout, 88
Potato Gorgonzola Gratin, 128
Roasted Turkey with Sweet
    Vegetable Purée, 68
Sausage, Sweet Potato and Apple
    Casserole, 52
Sweet and Russet Potato Latkes, 38
Turkey Kielbasa with Cabbage,
    Sweet Potatoes and Apples, 92
Walnut Sweet Potato Salad, 106
Arizona Turkey Stew, 182
Asian Dishes
Cauliflower and Potato Masala, 130
Curried Lamb Potato Salad, 118
Fish Tajin (Fish Braised in Olive
    Oil with Vegetables), 96
Garam Masala, 130
Malaysian Curried Beef, 70
Masaman Curry Beef, 74

Asian Dishes (*continued*)
Masaman Curry Paste, 74
Oriental Potato Salad, 116

B

Bacon
Beef Bourguignon, 70
Cheese & Bacon Potato Bake, 132
Cheesy Potato Skins, 8
Coq au Vin, 66
Corn and Onion Chowder, 172
German-Style Bratwurst &
    Sauerkraut, 94
Hot German Potato Salad, 108
Potato Skins with Cheddar Melt,
    10
Turkey Bacon Quiche in Tater
    Skins, 17
Warm Tomato-Potato Salad, 114
Western Omelet, 20
Baked Apple & Sweet Potato
    Casserole, 52
Baked Fish Galician Style, 100
Baked Fish with Potatoes and Onions,
    96
Baked Potatoes with Toppings
Beef Stroganoff and Zucchini
    Topped Potatoes, 60
Broccoli and Cheese Topped
    Potatoes, 58
Cheesy Broccoli Potatoes, 60
Colorado Potato Devils, 152
Double-Baked Potatoes, 144
Microwave Toluca Taters, 58
Bayou Yam Muffins, 42

Beef (*see also* **Sausage)**
Beef Bourguignon, 70
Beef Stroganoff and Zucchini
    Topped Potatoes, 60
Chili & Potato Casserole, 56
Cider Stew, 172
Classic Brisket Tzimmes, 76
Countdown Casserole, 48
Cowboy Kabobs, 78
Family Favorite Hamburger
    Casserole, 82
French Beef Stew, 173
Grilled Meat Loaves and Potatoes,
    78
Herb-Crusted Roast Beef and
    Potatoes, 72
Malaysian Curried Beef, 70
Masaman Curry Beef, 74
Meat and Potato Stir-Fry, 76
Oven-Easy Beef & Potato Dinner,
    50
Patchwork Casserole, 82
Potato-Crusted Meat Loaf, 80
Potato Topped Meat Loaf, 80
Savory Pot Roast, 72
Southwestern Potato Skins, 8
Spinach-Potato Bake, 50
Biscuits and Muffins
Bayou Yam Muffins, 42
Sweet Potato Biscuits, 40
Sweet Potato Pecan Muffins, 42
Bratwurst Skillet Breakfast, 30
Breakfast Hash, 32
Broccoli
Broccoli and Cheese Topped
    Potatoes, 58
Cheesy Broccoli Potatoes, 60

Broccoli (*continued*)
Ham & Potato Scallop, 54
Smoked Turkey and Fresh Vegetable Salad, 118
Brunswick Stew, 178

C

Cabbage and Sauerkraut
Bratwurst Skillet Breakfast, 30
Country Kielbasa Kabobs, 92
German-Style Bratwurst & Sauerkraut, 94
Kielbasa Kabobs, 94
Pork and Cabbage Ragout, 88
Turkey Kielbasa with Cabbage, Sweet Potatoes and Apples, 92
Caribbean Turkey Stew, 176
Casseroles
Baked Apple & Sweet Potato Casserole, 52
Baked Fish with Potatoes and Onions, 96
Cheese & Bacon Potato Bake, 132
Chili & Potato Casserole, 56
Classica™ Fontina Potato Surprise, 128
Countdown Casserole, 48
Creamy Scalloped Potatoes and Tuna, 51
Egg & Sausage Casserole, 28
Family Favorite Hamburger Casserole, 82
Festive Sweet Potato Combo, 136
Ham and Potato au Gratin, 48
Hash Brown Frittata, 25
Hearty Breakfast Custard Casserole, 28
Hearty Chicken Bake, 64
Oven-Easy Beef & Potato Dinner, 50
Patchwork Casserole, 82
Potatoes au Gratin, 124
Potatoes Jarlsberg, 126

Casseroles (*continued*)
Potato Gorgonzola Gratin, 128
Rosy Potato and Pepper Gratin, 133
Sausage, Sweet Potato and Apple Casserole, 52
Sausage and Potato Bake, 46
Savory Pork Chop Supper, 88
Scalloped Potatoes, 126
Scalloped Potatoes Nokkelost, 132
Spam™ Hash Brown Bake, 33
Spinach-Potato Bake, 50
Sunny Day Casserole, 44
Sweet 'n' Sassy Potato Casserole, 142
Tomato Scalloped Potatoes, 132
Cauliflower and Potato Masala, 130
Cheese
Broccoli and Cheese Topped Potatoes, 58
Cheese & Bacon Potato Bake, 132
Cheese and Pepper Stuffed Potato Skins, 6
Cheesy Broccoli Potatoes, 60
Cheesy Mashed Potatoes and Turnips, 134
Cheesy Potato Pancakes, 38
Cheesy Potato Skins, 8
Cheesy Potato Skins with Black Beans & Salsa, 10
Chili & Potato Casserole, 56
Classica™ Fontina Potato Surprise, 128
Classic Potato, Onion & Ham Pizza, 90
Colorado Potato & Prosciutto Salad, 116
Colorado Potato Devils, 152
Countdown Casserole, 48
Creamy Scalloped Potatoes and Tuna, 51
Double-Baked Potatoes, 144
Fennel and Potato Bisque, 160
Garden Frittata, 25
Golden Mashed Potatoes, 134
Ham and Potato au Gratin, 48

Cheese (*continued*)
Hash Brown Frittata, 25
Hearty Chicken Bake, 64
Mediterranean Montrachet® Salad, 122
Microwave Toluca Taters, 58
Oven-Easy Beef & Potato Dinner, 50
Patchwork Casserole, 82
Potato & Cheddar Soup, 164
Potato and Cheese Omelet, 24
Potato and Egg Pie, 30
Potato-Cheese Calico Soup, 170
Potato-Crusted Meat Loaf, 80
Potatoes au Gratin, 124
Potatoes Jarlsberg, 126
Potato Gorgonzola Gratin, 128
Potato Skins with Cheddar Melt, 10
Potato-Swiss Galette, 146
Rosy Potato and Pepper Gratin, 133
Rustic Potatoes au Gratin, 130
Scalloped Potatoes, 126
Scalloped Potatoes Nokkelost, 132
Seafood Bisque, 166
Southern Stuffed New Potatoes with Wisconsin Asiago, Ham and Mushrooms, 16
Southwestern Potato Skins, 8
Spam™ Hash Brown Bake, 33
StarKist® Swiss Potato Pie, 44
Stuffed Franks 'n Taters, 46
Sunny Day Casserole, 44
Sweet Potato Ravioli with Asiago Cheese Sauce, 102
Tamale Potato Quiche, 26
Tomato Scalloped Potatoes, 132
Wisconsin True Blue Potato Salad, 115
Zesty Potato Fillo Quiche, 24
Chicken
Brunswick Stew, 178
Chicken Pepper Pot Soup, 162
Chicken-Potato Pot Pie, 51
Chicken Potato Salad Olé, 114
Chicken Salad Niçoise, 122

Chicken (*continued*)
Chicken-Vegetable Skillet, 64
Chicken Vesuvio, 68
Coq au Vin, 66
Country Chicken Stew, 176
Creamy Shell Soup, 158
Glazed Chicken & Vegetable Skewers, 62
Hearty Chicken Bake, 64
Home-Style Chicken and Sweet Potato Stew, 180
Rocky Mountain Hash with Smoked Chicken, 62
Snappy Pea and Chicken Pot Pie, 63
Vesuvio Roasted Chicken and Potatoes, 66
Chili & Potato Casserole, 56
Chips, Potato
Herbed Potato Chips, 14
Homemade Potato Chips, 14
Hot & Spicy Ribbon Chips, 14
Spam™ Hash Brown Bake, 33
Cider Stew, 172
Cinnamon Applesauce, 37
Cinnamon Apple Sweet Potatoes, 140
Classica™ Fontina Potato Surprise, 128
Classic Brisket Tzimmes, 76
Classic Potato, Onion & Ham Pizza, 90
Classic Potato Salad, 118
Colorado Potato & Prosciutto Salad, 116
Colorado Potato Devils, 152
Coq au Vin, 66
Corn and Onion Chowder, 172
Countdown Casserole, 48
Country Chicken Stew, 176
Country Kielbasa Kabobs, 92
Country Skillet Hash, 32
Country-Style Mashed Potatoes, 134
Country-Style Potato Salad, 120

Country-Style Sausage Potato Salad, 106
Cowboy Kabobs, 78
Creamy Asparagus Potato Soup, 164
Creamy Corn Bisque with Spicy Red Pepper Cream, 168
Creamy Scalloped Potatoes and Tuna, 51
Creamy Shell Soup, 158
Curried Lamb Potato Salad, 118

D

Dijonnaise Potato Salad, 108
Dijon Vinaigrette, 104
Dilled New Potatoes and Peas, 154
Dilled Vichyssoise, 164
Double-Baked Potatoes, 144

E

Egg Dishes
Breakfast Hash, 32
Cheesy Potato Pancakes, 38
Egg & Sausage Casserole, 28
Frittata Primavera, 22
Garden Frittata, 25
Hash Brown Frittata, 25
Hearty Breakfast Custard Casserole, 28
Potato and Cheese Omelet, 24
Potato and Egg Pie, 30
Potato and Pork Frittata, 22
StarKist® Swiss Potato Pie, 44
Tamale Potato Quiche, 26
Turkey Bacon Quiche in Tater Skins, 17
Western Omelet, 20
Zesty Potato Fillo Quiche, 24

European Dishes (*see also* **French Dishes; Italian Dishes**)
Fish & Chips, 98
German-Style Bratwurst & Sauerkraut, 94
Hot German Potato Salad, 108
Irish Stew in Bread, 84
Mediterranean Montrachet® Salad, 122
Norse Skillet Potatoes, 150
Potatoes with Onions à la Smyrna, 154
Shepherd's Pie, 56
Swiss Rosti Potato Cake, 40

F

Family Favorite Hamburger Casserole, 82
Farmer's Market Salad, 120
Fennel and Potato Bisque, 160
Festive Sweet Potato Combo, 136
Fish and Seafood
Baked Fish Galician Style, 100
Baked Fish with Potatoes and Onions, 96
Creamy Scalloped Potatoes and Tuna, 51
Fish & Chips, 98
Fish Tajin (Fish Braised in Olive Oil with Vegetables), 96
Grilled Tuna Niçoise, 101
Kaleidoscope Chowder, 166
New England Fisherman's Skillet, 100
New West Crab Cakes, 98
Seafood Bisque, 166
StarKist® Swiss Potato Pie, 44
Vegetable and Shrimp Chowder, 158

French Dishes
Baked Fish Galician Style, 100
Beef Bourguignon, 70
Chicken Salad Niçoise, 122
Coq au Vin, 66
Dilled Vichyssoise, 164
French Beef Stew, 173
Grilled Tuna Niçoise, 101
Vichyssoise, 160
Frittata Primavera, 22

G

Garam Masala, 130
Garden Frittata, 25
German-Style Bratwurst &
    Sauerkraut, 94
Glazed Chicken & Vegetable Skewers,
    62
Glazes, Pastes and Dressings
Dijon Vinaigrette, 104
Golden Glaze, 62
Herb and Mustard Dressing,
    122
Honey Thyme Mustard, 146
Masaman Curry Paste, 74
Pesto Sauce, 112
Spice Paste, 174
Golden Apples and Yams, 136
Golden Glaze, 62
Golden Mashed Potatoes, 134
Gourmet Deli Potato & Pea Salad,
    110
Green Bean and Potato Salad in Dijon
    Vinaigrette, 104
Green Bean Potato Salad, 115
Grilled Dishes
Country Kielbasa Kabobs, 92
Cowboy Kabobs, 78
Glazed Chicken & Vegetable
    Skewers, 62
Grilled Cajun Potato Wedges, 148
Grilled Meat Loaves and Potatoes,
    78

Grilled Dishes (continued)
Grilled Pork and Potatoes Vesuvio,
    86
Grilled Tuna Niçoise, 101
Jamaican Grilled Sweet Potatoes,
    142
Kielbasa Kabobs, 94

H

Ham
Classica™ Fontina Potato Surprise,
    128
Classic Potato, Onion & Ham Pizza,
    90
Colorado Potato & Prosciutto
    Salad, 116
Garden Frittata, 25
Ham and Potato au Gratin, 48
Ham & Potato Scallop, 54
Maple Spam™ Stuffed Squash, 102
Potato & Cheddar Soup, 164
Southern Stuffed New Potatoes
    with Wisconsin Asiago, Ham and
    Mushrooms, 16
Spam™ Corn Chowder, 156
Spam™ Hash Brown Bake, 33
Sunny Day Casserole, 44
Sweet Potato and Ham Soup, 162
Hash Brown Potatoes
Countdown Casserole, 48
Egg & Sausage Casserole, 28
Family Favorite Hamburger
    Casserole, 82
Ham and Potato au Gratin, 48
Hash Brown Frittata, 25
Maple Spam™ Stuffed Squash, 102
Oven-Easy Beef & Potato Dinner,
    50
Patchwork Casserole, 82
Potato and Egg Pie, 30
Potato and Pork Frittata, 22
Potato-Zucchini Pancakes with
    Warm Corn Salsa, 36

Hash Brown Potatoes (continued)
Spam™ Hash Brown Bake, 33
StarKist® Swiss Potato Pie, 44
Stuffed Franks 'n Taters, 46
Hearty Breakfast Custard Casserole, 28
Hearty Chicken Bake, 64
Hearty Sausage Stew, 182
Herb and Mustard Dressing, 122
Herb-Crusted Roast Beef and
    Potatoes, 72
Herbed Potato Chips, 14
Homemade Potato Chips, 14
Home-Style Chicken and Sweet
    Potato Stew, 180
Honey Mustard Roasted Potatoes, 146
Honey Thyme Mustard, 146
Hot & Spicy Ribbon Chips, 14
Hot German Potato Salad, 108
Hot Sweet Potatoes, 138

I

Irish Stew in Bread, 84
Italian Dishes
Chicken Vesuvio, 68
Classica™ Fontina Potato Surprise,
    128
Classic Potato, Onion & Ham Pizza,
    90
Frittata Primavera, 22
Garden Frittata, 25
Grilled Pork and Potatoes Vesuvio,
    86
Sautéed Garlic Potatoes, 144
Sweet Potato Ravioli with Asiago
    Cheese Sauce, 102
Vesuvio Roasted Chicken and
    Potatoes, 66

J

Jamaican Black Bean Stew, 180
Jamaican Grilled Sweet Potatoes, 142

K

Kaleidoscope Chowder, 166
Kielbasa Kabobs, 94

L

Lamb
  Curried Lamb Potato Salad, 118
  Irish Stew in Bread, 84
  Lamb in Dill Sauce, 84
  Shepherd's Pie, 56
  Spicy Lamb & Potato Nests, 17
Latkes (Potato Pancakes), 36
Lawry's® Fiesta Dip, 8

M

Malaysian Curried Beef, 70
Maple Spam™ Stuffed Squash, 102
Masaman Curry Beef, 74
Masaman Curry Paste, 74
Mashed Potatoes
  Bayou Yam Muffins, 42
  Cheesy Mashed Potatoes and
    Turnips, 134
  Cheesy Potato Pancakes, 38
  Chili & Potato Casserole, 56
  Country-Style Mashed Potatoes,
    134
  Golden Mashed Potatoes, 134
  Hearty Chicken Bake, 64
  New West Crab Cakes, 98
  Pork and Cabbage Ragout, 88
  Potato Topped Meat Loaf, 80
  Roasted Garlic Mashed Potatoes, 133
  Santa Fe Potato Cakes, 150
  Spinach-Potato Bake, 50
  Sweet Potato Biscuits, 40
  Sweet Potato Gratin, 138
  Sweet Potato Pecan Muffins, 42
  Sweet Potato Soufflé, 140

Meat and Potato Stir-Fry, 76
Mediterranean Montrachet® Salad, 122
Microwave Dishes
  Bayou Yam Muffins, 42
  Cheesy Broccoli Potatoes, 60
  Cinnamon Apple Sweet Potatoes,
    140
  Countdown Casserole, 48
  Gourmet Deli Potato & Pea Salad,
    110
  Hot German Potato Salad, 108
  Microwave Toluca Taters, 58
  Stuffed Franks 'n Taters, 46
  Zesty Potato Fillo Quiche, 24
Mushrooms
  Arizona Turkey Stew, 182
  Beef Stroganoff and Zucchini
    Topped Potatoes, 60
  Chicken-Vegetable Skillet, 64
  Coq au Vin, 66
  Hearty Sausage Stew, 182
  Irish Stew in Bread, 84
  Potato-Cheese Calico Soup, 170
  Southern Stuffed New Potatoes
    with Wisconsin Asiago, Ham and
    Mushrooms, 16

N

New England Fisherman's Skillet, 100
New West Crab Cakes, 98
Norse Skillet Potatoes, 150
Nuts
  Masaman Curry Beef, 74
  New West Crab Cakes, 98
  Roasted Turkey with Sweet
    Vegetable Purée, 68
  Sweet Potato Biscuits, 40
  Sweet Potato Pecan Muffins, 42
  Sweet Potato Salad, 112
  Sweet Potato Soufflé, 140
  Walnut Sweet Potato Salad, 106
  Walnut Turkey Hash, 33

O

One Potato, Two Potato, 18
Oriental Potato Salad, 116
Oven-Easy Beef & Potato Dinner, 50

P

Pancakes, Potato
  Apple-Potato Pancakes, 34
  Cheesy Potato Pancakes, 38
  Latkes (Potato Pancakes), 36
  Potato Latkes with Cinnamon
    Applesauce, 37
  Potato Pancake Appetizers, 12
  Potato-Zucchini Pancakes with
    Warm Corn Salsa, 36
  Santa Fe Potato Cakes, 150
  Sweet and Russet Potato Latkes, 38
  Turkey Sausage Potato Pancakes, 34
Patchwork Casserole, 82
Pecos "Red" Stew, 173
Pesto Sauce, 112
Pork (see also Ham; Bacon; Sausage)
  Country Skillet Hash, 32
  Grilled Pork and Potatoes Vesuvio,
    86
  Pecos "Red" Stew, 173
  Pork and Cabbage Ragout, 88
  Potato and Pork Frittata, 22
  Savory Pork Chop Supper, 88
  Sweet Potato Cranberry Stew, 178
Potato & Cheddar Soup, 164
Potato and Cheese Omelet, 24
Potato and Egg Pie, 30
Potato and Pork Frittata, 22
Potato-Cheese Calico Soup, 170
Potato-Crusted Meat Loaf, 80
Potatoes au Gratin, 124
Potatoes Jarlsberg, 126
Potatoes with Onions à la Smyrna,
  154
Potato Gorgonzola Gratin, 128

Potato Latkes with Cinnamon Applesauce, 37
Potato Pancake Appetizers, 12
Potato Skins with Cheddar Melt, 10
Potato Sweets, 18
Potato-Swiss Galette, 146
Potato Topped Meat Loaf, 80
Potato-Zucchini Pancakes with Warm Corn Salsa, 36

Pot Pies
Chicken-Potato Pot Pie, 51
Shepherd's Pie, 56
Snappy Pea and Chicken Pot Pie, 63
StarKist® Swiss Potato Pie, 44
Sweet Potato Turkey Pie, 54

R

Ranch Picnic Potato Salad, 115
Roasted Garlic Mashed Potatoes, 133
Roasted Turkey with Sweet Vegetable Purée, 68
Rocky Mountain Hash with Smoked Chicken, 62
Rosemary Hash Potatoes, 152
Rosy Potato and Pepper Gratin, 133
Rustic Potatoes au Gratin, 130

S

Salsa
Cheesy Potato Skins with Black Beans & Salsa, 10
Warm Corn Salsa, 36
Santa Fe Potato Cakes, 150
Saucy Skillet Potatoes, 152

Sausage
Bratwurst Skillet Breakfast, 30
Breakfast Hash, 32
Country Kielbasa Kabobs, 92
Country-Style Sausage Potato Salad, 106

Sausage (continued)
Egg & Sausage Casserole, 28
German-Style Bratwurst & Sauerkraut, 94
Hash Brown Frittata, 25
Hearty Breakfast Custard Casserole, 28
Hearty Sausage Stew, 182
Kielbasa Kabobs, 94
Potato and Egg Pie, 30
Sausage, Sweet Potato and Apple Casserole, 52
Sausage and Potato Bake, 46
Skillet Franks and Potatoes, 90
Stuffed Franks 'n Taters, 46
Turkey Kielbasa with Cabbage, Sweet Potatoes and Apples, 92
Turkey Sausage Potato Pancakes, 34
Sautéed Garlic Potatoes, 144
Savory Pork Chop Supper, 88
Savory Pot Roast, 72
Savory Sweet Potato Sticks, 18
Scalloped Potatoes, 126
Scalloped Potatoes Nokkelost, 132
Seafood Bisque, 166
Shepherd's Pie, 56

Skillet Dishes
Bratwurst Skillet Breakfast, 30
Breakfast Hash, 32
Cheesy Potato Pancakes, 38
Chicken-Vegetable Skillet, 64
Country Skillet Hash, 32
Fish & Chips, 98
Fish Tajin (Fish Braised in Olive Oil with Vegetables), 96
Frittata Primavera, 22
Garden Frittata, 25
German-Style Bratwurst & Sauerkraut, 94
Homemade Potato Chips, 14
Hot & Spicy Ribbon Chips, 14
Latkes (Potato Pancakes), 36
Malaysian Curried Beef, 70
Masaman Curry Beef, 74

Skillet Dishes (continued)
Meat and Potato Stir-Fry, 76
New England Fisherman's Skillet, 100
New West Crab Cakes, 98
Norse Skillet Potatoes, 150
Potato and Cheese Omelet, 24
Potato-Swiss Galette, 146
Rosemary Hash Potatoes, 152
Santa Fe Potato Cakes, 150
Saucy Skillet Potatoes, 152
Sautéed Garlic Potatoes, 144
Skillet Franks and Potatoes, 90
Smoky Potato Salad, 110
Southern Smothered Potatoes, 148
Sweet and Russet Potato Latkes, 38
Swiss Rosti Potato Cake, 40
Turkey Kielbasa with Cabbage, Sweet Potatoes and Apples, 92
Turkey Sausage Potato Pancakes, 34
Walnut Turkey Hash, 33
Western Omelet, 20

Skins, Potato
Cheese and Pepper Stuffed Potato Skins, 6
Cheesy Potato Skins, 8
Cheesy Potato Skins with Black Beans & Salsa, 10
Potato Skins with Cheddar Melt, 10
Southwestern Potato Skins, 8
Turkey Bacon Quiche in Tater Skins, 17

Slow Cooker Dishes
Lamb in Dill Sauce, 84
Rustic Potatoes au Gratin, 130
Smoked Turkey and Fresh Vegetable Salad, 118
Smoky Potato Salad, 110
Snappy Pea and Chicken Pot Pie, 63
Southern Smothered Potatoes, 148
Southern Stuffed New Potatoes with Wisconsin Asiago, Ham and Mushrooms, 16
Southwestern Potato Skins, 8
Spam™ Corn Chowder, 156

Spam™ Hash Brown Bake, 33
Spice Paste, 174
Spicy African Chick-Pea and Sweet
    Potato Stew, 174
Spicy Lamb & Potato Nests, 17
Spinach
    Ham and Potato au Gratin, 48
    Kaleidoscope Chowder, 166
    Spinach-Potato Bake, 50
    Vegetable Soup, 156
StarKist® Swiss Potato Pie, 44
Stuffed Franks 'n Taters, 46
Sunny Day Casserole, 44
Sweet and Russet Potato Latkes, 38
Sweet 'n' Sassy Potato Casserole, 142
Sweet Potatoes and Yams
    Baked Apple & Sweet Potato
        Casserole, 52
    Bayou Yam Muffins, 42
    Caribbean Turkey Stew, 176
    Cinnamon Apple Sweet Potatoes,
        140
    Classic Brisket Tzimmes, 76
    Festive Sweet Potato Combo, 136
    Golden Apples and Yams, 136
    Home-Style Chicken and Sweet
        Potato Stew, 180
    Hot Sweet Potatoes, 138
    Jamaican Black Bean Stew, 180
    Jamaican Grilled Sweet Potatoes,
        142
    Potato Sweets, 18
    Roasted Turkey with Sweet
        Vegetable Purée, 68
    Sausage, Sweet Potato and Apple
        Casserole, 52
    Savory Sweet Potato Sticks, 18
    Spicy African Chick-Pea and Sweet
        Potato Stew, 174
    Sweet and Russet Potato Latkes,
        38
    Sweet 'n' Sassy Potato Casserole,
        142
    Sweet Potato and Ham Soup, 162
    Sweet Potato Biscuits, 40

Sweet Potato Cranberry Stew, 178
Sweet Potato Gratin, 138
Sweet Potato Pecan Muffins, 42
Sweet Potato Puffs, 140
Sweet Potato Ravioli with Asiago
    Cheese Sauce, 102
Sweet Potato Salad, 112
Sweet Potato Soufflé, 140
Sweet Potato Turkey Pie, 54
Turkey Kielbasa with Cabbage,
    Sweet Potatoes and Apples, 92
Walnut Sweet Potato Salad, 106
Swiss Rosti Potato Cake, 40

T

Tamale Potato Quiche, 26
Tex-Mex Dishes
    Arizona Turkey Stew, 182
    Cheesy Potato Skins with Black
        Beans & Salsa, 10
    Chicken Potato Salad Olé, 114
    Cowboy Kabobs, 78
    Double-Baked Potatoes, 144
    Lawry's® Fiesta Dip, 8
    Microwave Toluca Taters, 58
    Pecos "Red" Stew, 173
    Potato-Zucchini Pancakes with
        Warm Corn Salsa, 36
    Santa Fe Potato Cakes, 150
    Southwestern Potato Skins, 8
    Tamale Potato Quiche, 26
    Warm Corn Salsa, 36
    Western Omelet, 20
Three-Peppered Potatoes, 154
Tomato Scalloped Potatoes, 132
Turkey (*see also* **Sausage; Bacon**)
    Arizona Turkey Stew, 182
    Caribbean Turkey Stew, 176
    Microwave Toluca Taters, 58
    Roasted Turkey with Sweet
        Vegetable Purée, 68
    Smoked Turkey and Fresh Vegetable
        Salad, 118

Turkey (*continued*)
    Sweet Potato Turkey Pie, 54
    Walnut Turkey Hash, 33
Turkey Bacon Quiche in Tater Skins, 17
Turkey Kielbasa with Cabbage, Sweet
    Potatoes and Apples, 92
Turkey Sausage Potato Pancakes, 34

V

Vegetable and Shrimp Chowder, 158
Vegetable-Bean Chowder, 170
Vegetable Soup, 156
Vesuvio Roasted Chicken and
    Potatoes, 66
Vichyssoise, 160

W

Walnut Sweet Potato Salad, 106
Walnut Turkey Hash, 33
Warm Corn Salsa, 36
Warm Tomato-Potato Salad, 114
Western Omelet, 20
Wisconsin True Blue Potato Salad,
    115

Y

Yellow Couscous, 174

Z

Zesty Baked Red Potato Fans, 12
Zesty Potato Fillo Quiche, 24
Zucchini
    Beef Stroganoff and Zucchini
        Topped Potatoes, 60
    Potato Pancake Appetizers, 12
    Potato-Zucchini Pancakes with
        Warm Corn Salsa, 36

METRIC CONVERSION CHART

VOLUME MEASUREMENTS (dry)

1/8 teaspoon = 0.5 mL
1/4 teaspoon = 1 mL
1/2 teaspoon = 2 mL
3/4 teaspoon = 4 mL
1 teaspoon = 5 mL
1 tablespoon = 15 mL
2 tablespoons = 30 mL
1/4 cup = 60 mL
1/3 cup = 75 mL
1/2 cup = 125 mL
2/3 cup = 150 mL
3/4 cup = 175 mL
1 cup = 250 mL
2 cups = 1 pint = 500 mL
3 cups = 750 mL
4 cups = 1 quart = 1 L

VOLUME MEASUREMENTS (fluid)

1 fluid ounce (2 tablespoons) = 30 mL
4 fluid ounces (1/2 cup) = 125 mL
8 fluid ounces (1 cup) = 250 mL
12 fluid ounces (1 1/2 cups) = 375 mL
16 fluid ounces (2 cups) = 500 mL

WEIGHTS (mass)

1/2 ounce = 15 g
1 ounce = 30 g
3 ounces = 90 g
4 ounces = 120 g
8 ounces = 225 g
10 ounces = 285 g
12 ounces = 360 g
16 ounces = 1 pound = 450 g

DIMENSIONS

1/16 inch = 2 mm
1/8 inch = 3 mm
1/4 inch = 6 mm
1/2 inch = 1.5 cm
3/4 inch = 2 cm
1 inch = 2.5 cm

OVEN TEMPERATURES

250°F = 120°C
275°F = 140°C
300°F = 150°C
325°F = 160°C
350°F = 180°C
375°F = 190°C
400°F = 200°C
425°F = 220°C
450°F = 230°C

BAKING PAN SIZES

Utensil	Size in Inches/Quarts	Metric Volume	Size in Centimeters
Baking or	8 × 8 × 2	2 L	20 × 20 × 5
Cake Pan	9 × 9 × 2	2.5 L	23 × 23 × 5
(square or	12 × 8 × 2	3 L	30 × 20 × 5
rectangular)	13 × 9 × 2	3.5 L	33 × 23 × 5
Loaf Pan	8 × 4 × 3	1.5 L	20 × 10 × 7
	9 × 5 × 3	2 L	23 × 13 × 7
Round Layer	8 × 1 1/2	1.2 L	20 × 4
Cake Pan	9 × 1 1/2	1.5 L	23 × 4
Pie Plate	8 × 1 1/4	750 mL	20 × 3
	9 × 1 1/4	1 L	23 × 3
Baking Dish	1 quart	1 L	—
or Casserole	1 1/2 quart	1.5 L	—
	2 quart	2 L	—